PRESENTED TO:

....

BY:

....

DATE:

....

CHOOSE ADVENTURE

180 EPIC DEVOTIONS FOR BRAVE BOYS

GLENN HASCALL

BARBOUR **kidz**
A Division of Barbour Publishing

© 2021 by Barbour Publishing, Inc.

ISBN 978-1-64352-802-1

Published by Barbour Publishing, Inc., 1810 Barbour Drive, Uhrichsville, Ohio 44683, www.barbourbooks.com

Our mission is to inspire the world with the life-changing message of the Bible.

Member of the
Evangelical Christian
Publishers Association

Printed in the United States of America.

000660 0321 SP

INTRODUCTION

Every day when you wake up, you can ask yourself, will today be ordinary or adventurous? It doesn't mean you have to have amazing plans for the day. Even if you feel like nothing cool is going on in your life (and even if really hard or sad things are happening), you can make each day exciting by putting your focus on the best place it can be—on God! Ask Him to teach you more and more about Him as you read the Bible, pray, and worship Him throughout your day. Ask Him to help you build faith in Him that is huge and strong. Ask Him to show you the good things He wants you to do. As you pray this way every day, watch how God builds your faith and bravery to do what He has planned for you, in both good times and bad. He wants you to have the best kind of life, the life He designed you for, following the plans He has made that are unique and meant especially for you! To choose adventure means to choose God and all that He wants for you!

AARON

The Lord said to Aaron,
"Go to meet Moses in the desert." So he went.
EXODUS 4:27

Maybe you have an older brother. Sometimes older brothers like to talk about everything you do wrong. They don't like to listen to younger brothers. Aaron was Moses' older brother, but most people knew Moses. God made sure Aaron would listen to his younger brother. Aaron had grown up a slave in Egypt. Moses had grown up as the adopted grandson of Pharaoh, the Egyptian king.

Aaron was in his eighties when God asked him to find Moses. God had a big plan to save His people, and Aaron would be a part of that plan. His adventure would take him before Pharaoh, through the Red Sea, and out into the wilderness. He was with Moses when the ten plagues came upon Egypt. These included a day with frogs, a storm with hail, and a time when locusts ate all the food. God brought His people out of Egypt. Aaron watched God do it.

I want to be someone who pays attention when You do big things, God. Help me keep my eyes open. Help me praise You because You do great works.

ABEDNEGO

*At the end of ten days they looked even better. . .than all
the young men who had been eating the king's best food.*
DANIEL 1:15

Who wouldn't want an all-you-can-eat buffet? You could stuff yourself with pizza, chicken, and cookies. That would be awesome, right? The problem is too much of anything is just. . .too much. Abednego was one of many young men taken prisoner by a foreign king. Other prisoners were happy to eat at the king's buffet, but there were four men who asked if they could eat vegetables and drink water. Some people didn't think it was a good idea to turn down the king's offer of rich food.

What a surprise. The four were allowed to eat veggies and water. After ten days, they looked healthier than the other men who had been feasting on rich food. Veggies and water became their full-time diet. The king was very happy with Abednego and his friends. He thought they were ten times better than the wise men in his kingdom. God walked with Abednego into hard places and made things better.

*It's hard to stand up for what's right, Lord.
But that's what You want me to do. Help me
do the right thing because it's the right thing to do.*

ABEL

*Abel brought a gift of the first-born of his flocks and of the
fat parts. The Lord showed favor to Abel and his gift.*
GENESIS 4:4

.... ☆ ....

The world's first parents had two sons who grew up
together. Abel raised livestock. His brother, Cain, planted
seeds and raised plants. Abel honored God by giving Him
a gift from the best of his flock. God was pleased with
Abel's gift. Cain chose a different gift—from what he had
grown—and his gift did not please God.

These two brothers were raised in the same family.
They learned the same lessons and heard the same stories. But only one honored God the right way. God made
sure Abel knew he had made the right choice. But his
brother, Cain, was jealous. He wanted God to be pleased
with his gift too. Abel made sure he made a good choice
when he had the chance to make a good choice.

*You want me to make good choices. I will try. Would You
help me, God? I don't want to be jealous when I feel
bad because someone made a better choice.
Help me honor You the right way.*

ABRAM

*The Lord said to Abram, "Leave your country,
your family and your father's house,
and go to the land that I will show you."*
GENESIS 12:1

Abram was used to his name. He had the name for longer than many grandpas have their names. If anyone had called him by another name, he might not have answered. He probably wouldn't think they were really talking to him. That was before his first *God adventure*.

Abram lived in a place with a funny name—Ur. That was his home. That's where his family lived. But God told Abram to follow Him to a new place because He had a new plan. Guess what? Abram obeyed even when it didn't seem like a plan he would have made. He left his home when he was seventy-five years old. If Abram was going to follow God, he had a lot to learn. No one likes to wait, but God gave Abram plenty of time to grow into a new name.

*God, I am not always patient. Sometimes I want something,
and I don't want to wait. Help me grow into new
life living because You know my name.*

ABRAHAM

*"No more will your name be Abram. But your name
will be Abraham. For I will make you
the father of many nations."*
GENESIS 17:5

.... ☆ ....

Your name has a meaning, but your family might not have thought about the meaning before giving you that name. It was different when the Bible was written. A few people had their names changed—by God. Abram was one of those guys. When God gave him a new name, it came with a promise. He went from being a man with no children to a man who was the father of many nations. His new name? Abraham.

The new name showed that Abraham was growing to trust God. It showed that God's good plan would come true. It proved that God loved Abraham.

Abraham would have children. Great nations came from Abraham's family. God changed his name. God changed his future. God delivered a miracle. The adventure began when Abraham accepted the way God thought of him.

*Your plans are bigger than mine, Lord. They are better
and filled with greater adventure. Help me choose
to see myself the way You see me. I am loved,
forgiven, and a part of Your family.*

ABRAHAM'S SERVANT

Then the servant took ten of Abraham's camels and left.
He took with him all kinds of gifts from Abraham.
Then he went to the city of Nahor in Mesopotamia.
GENESIS 24:10

If you wanted to know more about Abraham and his family, you might learn from Eliezer of Damascus. He was Abraham's servant, and many believe he was the one who helped find a wife for Abraham's son Isaac.

Abraham's servant went to visit Abraham's family to see if someone was willing to go back with him to Abraham. The first person he met was Rebekah. He had prayed that God would help him find the right girl to be Isaac's wife. Rebekah was the answer to his prayer.

Eliezer had worked for Abraham a long time. He knew the God Abraham served. This God was the only One who could answer prayers. Abraham's servant didn't start or end his adventure on his own. Abraham sent him, God went with him, and he returned knowing God had answered his prayers.

Help me go where You want me to go, God. Help me do
what You want me to do. And when You answer my
prayer, help me remember You never left me.

ABSALOM

Then a man came to David with news, saying,
"The hearts of the men of Israel are with Absalom."
2 SAMUEL 15:13

King David loved his son Absalom. He was strong. People liked him. But Absalom was reckless. He thought the rules were for other people.

Many people thought he would be the next king. Absalom liked the idea. But Absalom killed his brother Amnon. King David sent Absalom away for a while. When he returned, he found people who wanted him to steal the kingdom from his dad.

Absalom did nothing to show that he loved God or was even willing to follow Him. He did nothing to show that he loved his dad and was willing to obey the king. He did nothing to show that he was sorry he had broken the rules. *He just wanted to be in charge.*

God had a bigger adventure for Absalom, but the young man paid no attention. God gave him a better choice, but Absalom thought *he* knew better. He was offered forgiveness, but he didn't care.

When You offer forgiveness, Lord, help me accept it.
Help it change me. Help me make better choices.

ACHISH

Then David got up and ran that day from Saul.
He went to Achish king of Gath.
1 SAMUEL 21:10

.... ✩ ....

King Saul was very angry with David. Saul was so angry he wanted to kill David. Saul chased. David ran. That's what brought David to Gath, where he stood before King Achish. The Philistines lived in Gath. Had David made a mistake?

David had killed the Philistine champion Goliath. He had won a battle for Israel when his greatest title was "shepherd boy." Achish could have killed David that day, but David asked for help. "This poor man cried, and the Lord heard him. And He saved him out of all his troubles" (Psalm 34:6).

God saved David from a foreign king. Achish was not a fan of Israel. He wanted to hurt them, but God stopped an angry king from doing anything to harm the man He promised would be Israel's next leader.

When it seems everyone is against me, help me
remember, Lord, that You can protect me and cause
other people to rethink their choices. May my
greatest adventures be with You—not against You.

ADAM

Then the Lord God made man from the dust of the ground.
And He breathed into his nose the breath of life.
Man became a living being.
GENESIS 2:7

The first man came to life. God did it. It was easy for Him. Adam enjoyed his time with God. He wasn't afraid. He wasn't embarrassed. In those earliest days, Adam hadn't broken any of God's laws. Adam gave the animals their names. He marveled at the sky day and night. This was supposed to be Adam's full-time adventure.

God made things easy. There was one law—*just one*. Adam was not to eat the fruit that grew on one particular tree in the middle of the Garden of Eden. God even told Adam why it was a bad idea. But when Adam and his wife, Eve, were tempted, they both ate the fruit of that tree. Suddenly they were afraid of God, they didn't want to be around Him, and they were embarrassed. Doing what God says you shouldn't do always leads away from the personal adventure He has planned for you.

Help me make the choice You ask me to make, God.
Help me agree that Your way is the best way.

AGABUS

While we were there a few days, a man who speaks for God named Agabus came down from the country of Judea.
ACTS 21:10

.... ☆ ....

Paul was famous. So was Barnabas. Agabus? Well, he's mentioned in just two verses. It's a good possibility you've never heard of him. Agabus was a rare New Testament prophet. He spoke for God.

Some history books say that Agabus followed Jesus when He was alive. Some believe he was at the Last Supper with Jesus. It is believed that he died following Jesus.

Jesus helped people every day, and futures were changed because of His help. Agabus was a man who was changed by knowing Jesus, and he brought a message from God to Paul. He said there would be a famine and that people would be very hungry. God's message was true, and it was delivered by a man who knew his best adventures included doing what God told him to do.

I don't have to be famous to follow You, God. I don't have to be strong or mighty. I just need to go where You go, tell others how great You are, and watch You work.

AHIMELECH

*[Ahimelech] said, "The sword is here that belonged
to Goliath the Philistine. . . . Take it, if you
will. For it is the only one here."*
1 SAMUEL 21:9

David would be king one day, but when Ahimelech is mentioned in the Bible, David was trying to stay away from King Saul. David's men were hungry. The group came to the city of Nob and found the priest Ahimelech. He was the city's religious leader in charge of the tabernacle.

Ahimelech gave David the sword of Goliath. He asked a few questions before giving David the bread prepared for worship in Nob. This bread was not used for everyday meals. It wasn't an easy decision to allow it to be used for food. The bread was to be a gift to God, but God had said His people should feed those in need. That helped the priest make his decision.

Ahimelech's adventure was showing mercy, feeding the hungry, and helping others. Not everyone agreed with his decision, but God used the priest to help when help was needed.

*Help me show mercy to others, God.
May I care for others the way You care for me.*

AMOS

These are the words of Amos, a shepherd.
AMOS 1:1

....

Amos didn't have a college degree. He wasn't the leader of a big city. He didn't rent space in an office building. He didn't have awards on a shelf. No one had given a banquet to celebrate what he had done. He was nobody special. He worked with sheep—and sheep were smelly. Yet God spoke to Amos. God gave him a message to share.

Amos said that the world had turned its back on God. The people who heard his message believed that some people had done that, but not Israel. Amos was clear—*everybody* had turned their back—and God was going to make some changes. If the people wouldn't listen to a shepherd, maybe they would listen to other prophets like Hosea and Isaiah. But *they didn't.*

Amos was given a big adventure. He was asked to leave his job caring for sheep and accept the job of caring for people. It must have been hard, because while sheep sometimes listened, the people didn't.

I want to listen to You, God. I want to really hear what You say. Help what I learn to change what I do.

ANANIAS

[Ananias] put his hands on Saul and said,
"Brother Saul. . . . The Lord has sent me so you might
be able to see again and be filled with the Holy Spirit."
ACTS 9:17

Ananias was minding his own business when God asked him to do something he thought was dangerous. A Pharisee had come to town. The man named Saul had hurt many people who followed Jesus. Now he was blind. God asked Ananias to go to Straight Street and find him. Ananias was supposed to put his hands on Saul. When he did, Saul would be able to see again.

Maybe Ananias thought it would be a good idea for Saul to remain blind. He argued with God, but finally he obeyed. Saul could see again, and he began following what Jesus had taught.

Ananias was not Saul, and his story would be different, but his adventure brought him face-to-face with a man who caused suffering yet learned that Jesus was more than enough to turn lives in a new direction.

Never let me think I know who can and can't be loved
by You, Lord. Help me love people You love
so maybe they will love You too.

ANDREW

Jesus was walking by the Sea of Galilee.
He saw Simon and his brother Andrew putting
a net into the sea. They were fishermen.
MARK 1:16

Andrew was a disciple of Jesus. He was a fisherman. Peter was his brother. When Jesus invited Andrew on the adventure of a lifetime, he followed. At night he would sit with the other disciples and listen to Jesus. During the day they traveled. Sometimes Jesus would heal or perform a different miracle.

Andrew had been waiting for Jesus. Earlier Andrew had followed John the Baptist. He heard all about Jesus before he met Him. Andrew made himself available, and he wanted to learn. He knew there was more to life than fishing, so it was an easy decision when Jesus said, "Follow Me. I will make you fish for men!" (Matthew 4:19). Andrew put down his fishing nets so he could share God's good news. Some people wanted to know more. This was Andrew's adventure because he had the courage to follow.

I want to love Jesus enough to share Him with others,
Lord. Help me love others enough to share Your
good plan. Help me say the right words.

APOLLOS

A Jew by the name of Apollos had come to Ephesus.
He was from the city of Alexandria. He could talk
to people about the Holy Writings very well.
ACTS 18:24

Apollos was a preacher. He was a good one. Some people thought he was the best. And that was the problem. Apollos was talking about Jesus—not himself. He wanted people to love God even if they didn't like him. Some people loved Apollos more than God.

Paul even asked, "Who is Apollos? Who is Paul? We are only servants owned by God. He gave us gifts to preach His Word. And because of that, you put your trust in Christ" (1 Corinthians 3:5).

Paul trusted Christ. Apollos trusted Christ. Both wanted other people to trust Christ. Both wanted people to see Jesus first, last, and always.

Like so many men of the Bible, Apollos wanted people to love and serve God and follow His Son, Jesus.

I can love You, God. I can love Your Son. Help me love other
people enough to tell them about You. They need to know
what You've said so they can learn who You are.

AQUILA

[Paul wrote,] Greet Priscilla and Aquila.
They worked with me for Christ.
ROMANS 16:3

.... ☆ ....

Aquila and his wife, Priscilla, made tents. That's what the apostle Paul did too. They were friends.

Making tents meant they got to talk to a lot of people who needed tents. Those people needed to know about Jesus. God used tentmakers to share a message everyone needed to hear.

Aquila traveled a lot. Can you guess what that means? He was always talking to new people who needed tents *and Jesus*. He and his wife talked to Apollos to help the preacher understand more about Jesus.

Aquila was willing to serve God without a special title, without a book written about his life, and without ever being in the spotlight. Aquila was useful to God because he was willing to be used by God. Being willing is very important. When we know who helps us, we know who should get the credit. Hint: *It's always God.*

I want to share what You've done, God. I don't want people to think I believe I can do anything without Your help.
May I ask for help, and may I always remember to thank You because You help me.

ASA

*Asa was faithful to the Lord with all
his heart for all his days.*
1 Kings 15:14

At the end of life many people will have a memorial stone on their grave. Carved on that stone will be words that tell people who read it what that person's life was like. Some words could be personal or even funny. King Asa could have been described like this: "He was faithful to the Lord with all his heart for all his days."

He was faithful. He did the right thing. He followed God. That's how people remembered this good king. Asa watched his father make mistakes and hurt people during the short time he was king. Asa wanted to do better. He didn't follow his dad's example. He followed God. He didn't hurt people. Asa helped people. He made good choices—not for a day, a week, or a year, but for life.

God helped Asa—and Asa accepted God's help. That was Asa's great adventure.

*You are faithful, God. You want me to be faithful too.
You have a home in my heart. Help me use my
heart to love You for the rest of my life.*

ASAPH

*Then on that day David first called upon Asaph
and his brothers to give thanks to the Lord.*
1 CHRONICLES 16:7

King David asked Asaph to do something he already loved
to do—praise God. It was Asaph's new job, but it was also
his passion. When you read the Bible, you will read twelve
psalms written by Asaph. While God is the One who
inspired everything you read in the Bible, He used Asaph
to be one of the writers.

Asaph's adventure began before King David ever
asked him to help the people learn to praise and worship
God. Asaph decided the best way to serve God was to
make sure people knew how good God was—even on bad
days. God was worth praising even when life wasn't fair.

This wasn't a part-time job. Asaph worked for King
David and King Solomon and used music to tell people
how good God is. His words are just as important today.

*You are a good God. You deserve praise. You want me
to worship You. Help me learn from Asaph, Lord.
Help me take the time to honor You in the
words I say to You, about You, and for You.*

BALAAM

*Balaam got up in the morning and got his donkey ready,
and went with the leaders of Moab.*
NUMBERS 22:21

.... ☆ ....

Balak, king of Moab, was afraid of the people of Israel. They had left Egypt and wandered in the wilderness. Balak was nervous. There were a lot of people. He heard about a man named Balaam who blessed and cursed people for money. King Balak wanted to hire Balaam to curse Israel. Somehow he thought this bad idea was a good one.

Balaam believed in many different gods. He didn't seem surprised when the real God told him he could say only what He told him to say. Balaam chose to obey God. The king wanted Balaam to curse Israel, but four times Balaam blessed them. *God told him to.*

God took care of Israel when they lived in Egypt, when they left Egypt, and when other nations saw them as an enemy. A big adventure started the day a man who would believe anything obeyed the believable God.

You're the mightiest of the mighty, God. You don't pay attention to those who would curse Your family when You want to bless them. You're the God I choose to believe.

BARABBAS

*Every year at the time of the special supper,
Pilate would let one person who was in prison go free.*
LUKE 23:17

He was a robber. He killed a man. He was in prison. Barabbas received a get-out-of-jail-free card. It wasn't because he did something right. It wasn't because he got time off for good behavior. It wasn't even because he spent enough time in jail and it was time to leave.

Jesus took his place. Pilate offered to let Jesus go free—or Barabbas could go free. Jesus healed people, fed people, and loved people. Barabbas hurt people, robbed people, and mistreated people. It should have been an easy decision. *It wasn't.* Jesus was sentenced to death. A robber was set free.

The adventure for this man who sinned might have been in asking why Jesus was killed. He had the opportunity to learn more about Jesus outside prison. We don't know if Barabbas became a Christian, but if he thanked anyone, it would be the One who gave His life for the freedom of a guilty man.

*I have done the wrong thing, God.
I am guilty, yet You set me free.*

BARAK

Deborah said to Barak, "Get up! For this is the day the Lord has given Sisera into your hands. See, the Lord has gone out before you." So Barak went down from Mount Tabor, and 10,000 men followed him.

<small>JUDGES 4:14</small>

Barak was nervous. He was a commander in the army, but he didn't want to go into battle alone. The enemy was cruel, and Barak wanted the prophet Deborah to help him face the enemy.

Barak led ten thousand men, and Deborah came with him. She told him that if she went with him, someone else would be honored for winning the battle. The battle was decided when a woman named Jael defeated Sisera, the leader of the opposing army.

It seems Barak trusted a human before he trusted God. He followed a good person instead of a good God. He believed in what he could see instead of the promise of an invisible God. Barak's adventure ended in a missed chance to trust God.

Just imagine how Barak's story could have been better.

Help me be wise enough to follow You, God. I want to love other people and go where You send me.

BARNABAS

Barnabas was a good man and full of the Holy Spirit and faith. And many people became followers of the Lord.
ACTS 11:24

When people think about the apostle Paul, they often think about Barnabas. These two men traveled a lot. They were missionaries who helped start churches. They were preachers who helped people learn about Jesus. They were friends.

Barnabas chose the adventure of being an encourager. He did what many people don't want to do. Paul was grateful. Barnabas walked beside Paul, defended him, and stayed with him during some very hard days.

He was a good friend and loved Paul enough to tell him the truth. Paul needed Barnabas, and Barnabas helped Paul.

There's a lot to learn from Barnabas. He didn't need the spotlight to be used by God. He didn't leave his friend Paul when they disagreed. He didn't stop encouraging others when it would have been easy to be discouraged. We can all learn something from perhaps the best friend Paul ever had.

I want to be a friend like Barnabas, God. I want to be someone who encourages. Help me refuse to make people feel bad by saying words that are unkind.

BARTIMAEUS

*A blind man was sitting by the road.
He was asking people for food or money as
they passed by. His name was Bartimaeus.*
MARK 10:46

Bartimaeus was blind. He begged from those who lived in a world of light for food he ate in the dark. He asked for money from those who could work to help him because he could not work. What else could he do?

One day Jesus walked along the same road where Bartimaeus sat. When he was sure it was Jesus, Bartimaeus called out for help. People around him saw a beggar and told him to be quiet. Jesus said Bartimaeus should come to Him. *He did.* Jesus asked him what he wanted. Bartimaeus told Him he wanted to see. His faith helped him see.

This blind man saw the faces of the crowd, his own hands, and most amazing of all, Bartimaeus saw Jesus. His adventure began the day he called out to Jesus.

Jesus always answers.

*When I need help, I should call out to You, God.
You have answers when I have questions. You offer
hope when I think there is none. You are amazing.*

BARZILLAI

Barzillai was eighty years old. He had given food to the king while he stayed at Mahanaim, for he was a very rich man.
2 SAMUEL 19:32

King David's son Absalom tried to become king instead of his dad. This was a difficult time for David because it meant he would need to leave town.

Where did he go? To the home of his friend Barzillai. His friend was old. His friend was rich. Most of all, his friend was kind. David stayed with Barzillai for a while.

Barzillai took care of the king. Whatever David needed, Barzillai got. And when the time came for David to return home, his friend refused to simply tell him, "All the best." He went with David to make sure he safely crossed the Jordan River on the way home.

This man from Gilead showed kindness to King David. That was a starting place for a great adventure remembered in the Bible.

Help me not to be rude to others, Lord. I don't want the words I say and the things I do to hurt people who wonder if You're real. Help me show them what You look like in my words and actions.

BENJAMIN

The sons of Rachel were Joseph and Benjamin.
GENESIS 35:24

Abraham had a son named Isaac. Isaac had a son named Jacob. Jacob had a wife named Rachel. Together they had two sons—Joseph and Benjamin.

Benjamin had ten older half brothers. They didn't seem to want anything to do with Joseph and Benjamin.

After a while the rain stopped falling. The ground became dry. No crops would grow. Benjamin watched his older brothers begin a journey to Egypt. Their father heard there was food they could buy there. When his stepbrothers returned, they had a message they didn't want to share. If the family wanted more food from Egypt, then Benjamin would have to come with them the next time. Egypt's second-in-command had told them that was the only way they could buy food the next time.

Benjamin's adventure began when he took that first step toward Egypt. At the end of the long walk, he found out that the man who said he must come to Egypt was his long-lost brother Joseph.

I want to remember that You know things I don't, God. There is a reason for everything You do. Help me never forget that You love me.

BEZALEL

Bezalel, the son of Uri, son of Hur, of the family of Judah, made all that the Lord had told Moses.
EXODUS 38:22

Bezalel was an artist. He was chosen to help create the things God needed in His tabernacle. *Tabernacle* is the word used to describe a temple or church that could be moved like a tent. It didn't stay in one place forever.

Bezalel was in charge of making the ark of the covenant. This was a box made of gold that would stay in the holiest place in the tabernacle. It would hold things that meant something to God and His people—the stone tablets with the Ten Commandments on them, Aaron's rod, and some of the manna God gave the people to eat in the wilderness. Everything God said was needed, Bezalel and his artist friends made.

Adventure days began when Bezalel used the skills God gave him to help make the very things God needed made.

Take what I can do and use it if You want, God. Help me always give You all that I am. When You ask me to do something, I want to say yes.

BOAZ

Boaz took Ruth. She became his wife.
RUTH 4:13

Boaz was a successful farmer. Most of his time was spent preparing soil, planting seeds, or harvesting crops. That was before Ruth came to town. She was once married, but her husband had died. Her mother-in-law, Naomi, once lived in Bethlehem. When she returned, Ruth came with her.

The two women didn't have money to buy food, so Ruth went to the fields that Boaz had planted. She gathered leftover grain to make bread. There was something about Ruth that captured the attention of Boaz. He did all the right things to bring honor to God.

After they were married, Boaz and Ruth had a son named Obed. Obed was the father of David. David became the greatest king in Israel. God took something bad (the loss of a husband) and turned it into something good (the birth of a king). Boaz is remembered for his compassion. His life is remembered for doing the difficult thing when help was needed.

You are a good God with good plans. I don't always recognize Your goodness when I first find it, God. Help me see it and celebrate with You.

CAIN

*The day came when Cain brought a gift of
the fruit of the ground to the Lord.*
GENESIS 4:3

The first human baby ever born was Cain. Animals may have turned their heads to the side when they heard him cry. This was a new sound. His was a new voice.

Cain became a very good farmer. His brother Abel became a shepherd. Both were preparing to sacrifice to God. Abel brought his best livestock. Cain just put some of his produce together and thought it was enough.

Abel's sacrifice was just right. Cain's sacrifice was less than his best, and God noticed. Cain got angry. The boy who was born first became the first person to kill someone else. Cain killed his brother Abel because he was jealous.

God sent Cain away. Adam and Eve lost both sons. Everyone was sad.

Cain's adventure didn't last long. He went from being a talented farmer to a man who wandered from one place to the next remembering how anger led to the loss of relationships.

*I never want to be so angry that I hurt others, Lord.
Help my adventure with You to be filled
with kindness and forgiveness.*

CALEB

Then Caleb told the people in front of Moses to be quiet.
And he said, "Let us go up at once and take the land.
For we are well able to take it in battle."
NUMBERS 13:30

Twelve men were on a mission. God had promised the people of Israel a place to call their own. Moses sent the spies to see what could be seen. The mission wasn't supposed to try to prove God was wrong, but that's what happened.

Only two men came back from the mission saying, "Let us go up at once and take the land." The other ten? They were afraid. The people sided with the fearful spies. Caleb was one of the courageous spies. God made sure that when it was time to move into the land, Caleb and his fellow spy Joshua would have a home. The ten fearful spies were not rewarded for their fear.

Caleb's adventure meant that he trusted God even when most other people did not.

Like Caleb, I've been given a mission too, God.
Help me go where You lead, because I will never
be alone, even when few people follow.

CENTURION

*When the captain heard of Jesus, he sent some Jewish
leaders to Him. They were to ask if He would
come and heal this servant.*

LUKE 7:3

······································· ☆ ·······································

A centurion was a leader or captain of one hundred soldiers. He told soldiers what to do and watched those soldiers do what they were told to do.

A certain centurion needed Jesus' help. His servant was very sick. This centurion was a Roman soldier, and Jesus was a Jew. Most Jews did not want Rome to be in charge. But this soldier believed Jesus could help him. *He could.*

Jesus was almost to the centurion's house when someone met them and told Jesus not to bother making the trip. This soldier and leader of men did not think he was worthy to have Jesus come to his house. He asked if Jesus would just say that his servant was healed. The centurion believed it would happen. *It did.*

The centurion's adventure was believing Jesus could do what seemed impossible for people who didn't deserve it.

*You cared for me even when I didn't know You, God.
Thank You. Help me get to know You better
so I can care for You too.*

CLEOPAS

One of them, whose name was Cleopas, said to Him,
"Are you the only one visiting Jerusalem who has not
heard of the things that have happened here these days?"
LUKE 24:18

Two people were walking on the road to Emmaus. They were interested in the life of Jesus, but now they were very sad. Jesus had been crucified. While Cleopas and his friend were talking about Jesus, a man joined them on their walk.

They told this man everything they had heard about Jesus. They heard that Jesus rose from the dead, but that seemed hard to believe. The man shared what he knew about what the messenger prophets had said about Jesus. Cleopas liked talking with this man. Imagine his surprise when he learned that the man he had been talking to was actually Jesus!

One of the best adventures *ever* happened when Cleopas spoke with Jesus after He rose from the dead. He walked with Him, heard from Him, and asked Him questions.

I'm glad I can ask You anything, God. The best answers
are in the Bible. The best hope is in Your Son.
My best life is walking with You.

CORNELIUS

They said, "Cornelius sent us. He is a captain and a good man and he honors God. . . . He asks you to come to his house. He wants to hear what you have to say."
ACTS 10:22

Jesus said He came to rescue every person willing to be rescued. Most people thought He meant every person who was willing *and also Jewish*. Jesus meant *every* willing person.

Cornelius was not Jewish. He was a soldier. He worked for the Roman government. He was also one of the first people who was not Jewish to follow Jesus. God told Cornelius to find Peter. God told Peter that people who weren't Jews would be welcome in His family. Cornelius was proof.

Peter came to see Cornelius. After hearing what the soldier had to say, Peter replied, "I can see, for sure, that God does not respect one person more than another" (Acts 10:34).

This adventure was all about believing that what Jesus said was true and accepting God's unexpected gift of rescue.

I need to be rescued, Lord. I need to believe only You can do what I cannot. I need to believe You love me that much.

CUPBEARER

One night both the cup-carrier and the bread-maker of the king of Egypt had a dream while they were in prison.
GENESIS 40:5

.... ☆ ....

When you work for the king, you do your job the best you possibly can. If you are the baker, you bake bread. If you are the cupbearer, you make sure the king is refreshed with something to drink.

The cupbearer made the Egyptian king unhappy. He was sent to prison. Joseph (Jacob's son) was also in prison. The cupbearer had been in prison a long time. One night he dreamed a very strange dream. He asked Joseph if he knew what it meant.

The cupbearer told him the dream included a cup, grapes, and making sure the king wasn't thirsty. God told Joseph what the dream meant. The cupbearer got his old job back. When the time was right, the cupbearer told the king all about Joseph, and he got out of prison too.

The adventure of the cupbearer was knowing that even in very bad situations God can help people and answer prayers.

No matter where I go, God, You go with me.
No matter how hard things get, You can help.

CYRUS

"This is what Cyrus king of Persia says: 'The Lord, the God of heaven, has given me all the nations of the earth. He has chosen me to build Him a house in Jerusalem, which is in Judah.' "

Ezra 1:2

The people of Israel were taken from their homes. They had to live in a different country. They had to follow different rules. They wanted to go home, but some homes had been destroyed. Others sat empty. Would there be much to go back to?

Then came King Cyrus. He listened when people talked about Israel. He saw the sadness of the people. He started rebuilding the temple in Jerusalem so there would be a place of worship when the people returned home.

Some people thought this was a bad idea, but Cyrus felt that he had been chosen by God to rebuild. He believed the people who had been taken from their homes would return.

The courageous adventure for King Cyrus was in obeying God to make things better for other people.

Help me care about other people, God. May I be kind and helpful. May You give me a passion to serve.

DANIEL

*Then Daniel showed that he could do better work
than the other leaders and captains because a
special spirit was in him. So the king planned
to give him power over the whole nation.*
DANIEL 6:3

.... ☆ ....

Daniel was taken from Israel to Babylon as a young man. Most of his life was spent in Babylon, but Daniel never forgot God. *And God never forgot Daniel.*

One day there was a new law that people were supposed to follow. No one could pray to anyone but the king for a month. If they did, they would spend time with hungry lions.

Men who didn't like Daniel asked the king to make this rule. The king liked Daniel but didn't ask him what he thought about the new law.

Daniel was found praying to God. The king was sad but sent Daniel to the lions. God kept the lions' mouths closed. The king was happy. God rescued Daniel.

The adventure Daniel experienced came about as he watched God help him do the right thing and rescue him when others did the wrong thing.

*Give me courage to do the right thing, God.
Give me strength. Rescue me when I need help.*

DAVID

"The Lord has found a man who is pleasing to him in every way. He has chosen him to rule over his people, because you have not obeyed the Lord."
1 SAMUEL 13:14

You probably know about King David. He defeated Goliath. A boy defeated a giant. It's a good story. But it's not the only good story about David.

David was a shepherd and a good friend, and he was kind. He fought in battles, respected the king, and loved God. David was brave, patient, and joyful. He was also unfaithful, a murderer, and a liar.

David was not perfect, but when he broke God's law, he came to God and admitted he was wrong. David was someone who pleased God—not because he sinned, but because he didn't run away from God. He kept returning. He had the desire to follow God and honor Him. David was a shepherd. *He knew how to care for others.* He was a king. *He knew the responsibility of leading.* He followed God. *He knew there was a better direction.* Seeking God was always David's big adventure.

If I seek, You can be found, God.
Help me always come back when I run away.

DEMETRIUS

Everyone speaks good things about Demetrius.
The truth itself speaks for him. We say the same thing
also and you know we are speaking the truth.
3 JOHN 1:12

Demetrius seems like someone who would be a good friend. He seems trustworthy. He seems truthful. His name is mentioned by John only one time. People who study the Bible think Demetrius was the man John trusted to deliver his letters. See? He was a good friend who could be trusted to deliver truth.

Maybe you've never heard of Demetrius, but there was a time when many people knew him, and they believed he was a man worthy of honor. God honored Demetrius by making sure people knew that he did what God asked him to do.

Demetrius had the great adventure of doing what God asked—big things, small things, and in-between-sized things. He was faithful. People noticed. They told their friends. God was honored in the things Demetrius did.

I want people to say good things about me, God.
I want people to know that You have taught me well.
Remind me that I can be faithful to You because
You have always been faithful to me.

DIONYSIUS

Some people followed [Paul] and became Christians.
One was Dionysius, a leader in the city.
Acts 17:34

·································· ☆ ··································

Dionysius lived in Athens. He was a city leader. When Paul came to tell the people of Athens about Jesus, Dionysius was one of those who listened. He had probably heard about Jesus before, so he would have been interested in what Paul had to say.

While others were confused, Dionysius understood some things and learned new things. Dionysius didn't miss his chance, and he didn't wait. He became a Christian. Others did too.

Something amazing happens when someone finally sees that they need Jesus. It changes his life. When one person really follows Jesus, more people will want to know Jesus. And that was the great adventure Dionysius found himself on. He went from being a leader in the city to being a leader in the church. His love for Jesus helped others want to know more about the God who rescues.

Because You love me, Lord, help me show other people
Your love. I want other people to follow where You lead.
I want them to love others because You loved them first.

EHUD

But when the people of Israel cried to the Lord, the Lord gave them someone to save them. He gave them Ehud.
JUDGES 3:15

Life was hard for the people of Israel. Some thought they brought the difficulty on themselves. Kings from other countries fought against Israel, and one of the worst was Eglon, king of Moab. The people had struggled with this country for eighteen years, and they'd had enough. They asked God for help. *God sent Ehud.*

God made it possible for Ehud to take back land that the people of Moab had taken. He defeated an army of thousands. The things Ehud did helped Israel live peacefully for more than eight decades.

The people needed a hero, and while Ehud went to battle for the people, it was God who answered the prayers of His people and encouraged Ehud to help.

Ehud's great adventure was being an answer to prayer as he followed the God who answers prayer.

It would be wonderful to be an answer to someone's prayer, God. When people pray to You, please help me to be willing to be used to do something for those who need You.

ELI

*Eli answered, "I did not call you,
my son. Lie down again."*
1 SAMUEL 3:6

.... ☆ ....

Eli was a priest. Every day he served God. He spoke with people and listened to prayers. One day a woman named Hannah was praying. She needed God's help. She wanted a son. She promised that if she had a son, she would lend the boy to God.

God answered Hannah's prayer, and young Samuel was introduced to Eli. Samuel came to live in God's house. He was an encouragement to Eli.

It was rare for God to speak to people in those days, but God spoke to Samuel. The boy had never heard God's voice before. When God called, Samuel thought he was hearing Eli. The priest knew he hadn't called Samuel. It must have been God. Eli helped Samuel understand that God was talking to him and he should listen.

Eli's great adventure was helping Samuel grow from a mother's answered prayer to God's messenger prophet. Young Samuel needed help. Eli helped Samuel.

Make me an answer to prayer, God. When someone needs something, use me to help them. Make me willing.

ELIJAH

Then Elijah said to the people, "I am the only man left who speaks for God."
1 KINGS 18:22

.... ☆ ....

Sometimes it can seem like you are the only person who thinks God is worth following. It can be discouraging to think no one else wants to follow God. That's what it was like for Elijah. He followed God. He felt alone. He thought that if he died there would be no one left to remember God.

Even when Elijah showed King Ahab how powerful God was, he thought he was the only one left who spoke for God. But *God knew the truth*. There were others who followed. And even if there weren't, God only needs one person willing to obey to help someone else see that He's real.

Elijah's adventure was obeying God when it seemed like no one else would, standing up for what he believed when it would have been easier to sit quietly, and knowing that even if he was alone, God had given him a job to do.

Help me speak for You, God. Let me help others see that You change things when we ask for help.

ELIPHAZ THE TEMANITE

[Job's three friends] were Eliphaz the Temanite, Bildad the Shuhite, and Zophar the Naamathite. They agreed to meet together to come to share Job's sorrow and comfort him.
JOB 2:11

People need good friends. You do too. Job needed good friends when it seemed everything was falling apart. Three friends came to share Job's sorrow and to comfort him. That's what they wanted to do, but they just couldn't.

Eliphaz sat quietly for several days, but then he couldn't help offering advice. He blamed Job for all the problems he faced. Eliphaz said things that weren't true—things that were unkind. The Lord said to Eliphaz the Temanite, "My anger burns against you and your two friends, because you have not spoken of Me what is right, as My servant Job has" (Job 42:7).

Eliphaz thought he was doing the right thing, but a better adventure would have been to worship God and let Him help Job endure the struggles he faced.

I don't need to have all the answers, God. You have them. Help me ask You for answers and make sure other people know they can ask You for help when they don't know the right thing to do.

ELISHA

*The king was talking with Gehazi, the servant of
the man of God, saying, "Tell me all the
great things that Elisha has done."*
2 KINGS 8:4

God used Elisha to do great things. The king wanted a
progress report. Elisha's servant told the king about *miracles*, *healings*, and *helping others*. The story the king heard
included all three.

The *miracle* was a boy who was born into a family that
helped Elisha. The *healing* was for the same boy several
years later. The *helping hand* was just about to happen.
The same family that had experienced the miracle and
the healing had gone to live in another country for seven
years. Nothing would grow, and they needed food. Now
that plants grew again, they came back. They needed
help to get back their house and land. Elisha's progress
report allowed the king the opportunity to lend a hand to
a widow and her son.

Elisha's adventure meant he worked with widows and
kings. Mostly, Elisha worked with the God who knew that
widows and kings would need His help.

*Other people need Your help, Lord. Help me tell them
how You have helped me and the people I know.*

ENOCH

*Enoch walked with God, and he was
seen no more, for God took him.*
GENESIS 5:24

Enoch's name is written in the "Faith Hall of Fame" in Hebrews 11. The Bible doesn't say much about Enoch. He was the father of Methuselah. He was also the great-grandfather of Noah. He lived a long time, and he didn't die. "He pleased God" (Hebrews 11:5), he "walked with God," and "God took him" (Genesis 5:24).

God never explains what it looked like when He took Enoch, but what we need to know is that this man found a relationship with God to be more important than anything else. This pleased God.

Enoch's great adventure is found in these four words—*he walked with God*. This description sums up the kind of man he was and what he thought was most important—God. He didn't just think about God. Enoch walked with God. He wanted to know God. *He did.*

Walk with God. Know Him. Go.

*I want to be remembered as a person who walked with
You, God. Someday I will get to meet You face-to-
face, and I want to know You well enough that
it will seem like I'm meeting my best friend.*

EPAPHRAS

*You heard the Good News through our much-loved
brother Epaphras who is taking my place.
He is a faithful servant of Christ.*
COLOSSIANS 1:7

Epaphras was someone who worked with the apostle Paul. He's someone worth talking about—and not just because his name is fun to say. Epaphras encouraged others. He knew that people struggle, and he didn't want to see people discouraged. Epaphras shared the good news about Jesus. The apostle Paul relied on this man to help in the work God had given them to do.

We don't know what Epaphras said, but we know that what he did say helped other people We don't know what he did, but we know that what he did honored God.

People loved Epaphras. He was committed to the people he served. God loved Epaphras. He was committed to using him. Paul loved Epaphras. He was committed to watching him grow.

Epaphras lived the great adventure God had for him because he listened, obeyed, and grew in his faith.

*Help me become someone who hears what You say, God.
Help me do what You need done. When I listen and
obey, I shouldn't be surprised when I grow.*

EPHRAIM

*[Joseph gave his] second son the name of Ephraim.
"For," he said, "God has given me children
in the land of my suffering."*
GENESIS 41:52

Joseph had been sold as a slave in Egypt. But God was with Joseph. You'll read his story later. You should know that while in Egypt, Joseph got married and had two sons—Ephraim and Manasseh.

The name Ephraim means "fruitful." Other words that could be used to explain his name include *useful*, *rewarding*, and *successful*.

Jacob wanted to bless his grandsons. Joseph thought his father was confused because he blessed Ephraim before Manasseh. Ephraim was not the first son born to Joseph. People always blessed the first son. But Jacob insisted that Ephraim be the first to be blessed.

Ephraim's adventure may have started with being humble and undemanding. This is the kind of person God wants you to be, and it's just the kind of person God likes to bless.

You love the firstborn in every family, God. But You also love the second and each one after that. Help me remember You bless every member of Your family. No one is left out.

ESAU

Esau said to Jacob, "Let me eat some of that red meat, for I am very hungry."
GENESIS 25:30

Esau liked the outdoors. He hunted. He was hairy. He probably had a big voice. Once, after a long day of hunting, he found his twin brother, Jacob, making some stew. All Esau knew was that he was hungry—and he wanted a bowl full of tasty food from Jacob's cooking pot.

Jacob told his brother that he would trade him all the stew he could eat for his birthright. That meant that when their father died, *Jacob* would get everything that *Esau* was supposed to get. Esau was hungry. He didn't think things through very well. He took the stew.

Esau's adventure was less adventurous because he forgot to think about the consequences of making quick decisions. Things would have gone much better if he had asked God for wisdom. That would have honored God, and he would have made better choices.

I want You to make me wise, God. I want to know what You have to say about the things I want to do. Help me understand that Your way is always the best way.

ETHIOPIAN EUNUCH

He stopped the wagon. Then both Philip and the man from Ethiopia went down into the water and Philip baptized him.
ACTS 8:38

There once was a man from Ethiopia. He had been traveling. While he traveled, he read God's Word. He read of a man who came like a lamb. People were ashamed of him. The man would die. Something about the story made the Ethiopian sad. He wanted to know more.

Then he met the apostle Philip, who asked if he understood what he was reading. *He didn't.* Philip sat down beside the Ethiopian and told him all about Jesus. *It made sense.* He wanted to follow Jesus. *How could he take the next step?*

Could anything keep him from being baptized? Philip thought it was a good idea.

The Ethiopian man just encountered a great adventure. He didn't think twice about following Jesus. When he knew the truth, he changed directions. His journey with Jesus started the day Philip told him the truth about the God who rescues.

Sometimes people are ready to hear about You, God. Help me stand for You and tell the world just how good You are.

EUNUCHS

*Esther was taken to the king's house
into the care of Hegai.*
ESTHER 2:8

You've probably never heard of Hegai, Shaashgaz, Hathach, or Harbona. These were all eunuchs who worked for King Xerxes. He was the king who made Esther his queen.

Each eunuch had a special job to do. Each helped the king with a specific job. At least two of these eunuchs were also helpful to Queen Esther. Their job was to look out for the interests of the king and his family. They were good at their jobs. They helped identify threats to the king and queen. They helped them look their best.

Eunuchs had their own job to do, but they also had to work together. That's just like the Christian life. God has something for each person to do, but everyone works together to get God's job done. *God made it that way.*

The eunuchs' adventure was in knowing who they served and then doing their best to work with others to serve them well.

*Help me be trustworthy to do my best for
You, Lord. I want to honor You by doing
what needs to be done for You.*

EUTYCHUS

A young man named Eutychus sat in the window.
As Paul kept on preaching, this man started to go to sleep.
ACTS 20:9

Many people had come to hear the apostle Paul preach. Eutychus was a young man who found a spot at the window. As Paul preached, Eutychus fell asleep. When he did, he fell out of the window and dropped three floors to the ground. By the time anyone reached him, Eutychus was dead.

The crowd was sad and a little afraid, but when Paul arrived he said Eutychus was not dead. He picked the man up and life returned to him. The people stayed up the rest of the night talking about Jesus and finding ways to worship Him. Eutychus was wide awake now. He joined them.

In the morning Eutychus went home, praising God for His goodness. The other people left doing the same thing.

The great adventure for this young man was in being a miracle and then spending time praising the God who heals.

Your Son is known as the Great Physician. Lord, I want You
to heal the broken parts in me. Make my soul healthy.
Give me Your prescription for good health.

EZEKIEL

[God] said to [Ezekiel], "Son of man,
stand on your feet, and I will speak with you."
EZEKIEL 2:1

Daniel, Shadrach, Meshach, and Abednego had all been taken to live in Babylon. People had sinned, and a time-out in another country was the way God would convince them to listen to Him.

Ezekiel also lived in Babylon. He was one of God's messenger prophets. He had a lot to say. The people were in Babylon for one reason. God told Ezekiel, "Son of man, I am sending you to the sons of Israel, to sinful people who have turned against Me. They and their fathers have sinned against Me" (Ezekiel 2:3).

A big adventure was waiting for Ezekiel. He had a message to share that was important to God. This message made some people angry and caused others to laugh. Even when the news was bad, Ezekiel could trust it because God had also made some very good promises that meant very Good News.

Help me trust that when You make a promise, God,
You deliver. I can live with some bad news
when I know You will lead me through.

EZRA

[Ezra] was a writer who knew well the Law of Moses which the Lord God of Israel had given. The king gave him everything he asked for, because the Lord his God was good to him.
EZRA 7:6

Ezra was a priest. It seemed like he was out of work—but he wasn't. The temple in Jerusalem was broken down and empty. He was taken from his home and made to live with people who didn't honor God. But the job God had for this messenger prophet didn't require a building. The words Ezra would speak just needed ears to hear and a mind to learn truth.

Because he was a priest, Ezra talked about God. Because he was a writer, he wrote down what God was teaching him. Because he loved God, Ezra stood strong when others didn't want to follow God.

Ezra's adventure took courage, patience, and love. He had to care about other people so much that he told the truth about God even when it seemed everyone else had forgotten God's goodness.

Help me be patient with people who don't love You, God. Help me love them enough to keep sharing the truth.

FELIX

Then Felix, the leader of the people, told Paul to speak.
Acts 24:10

The name Felix meant "to be happy," but Felix was not happy. He worked for the government, and he kept making bad decisions. He was cruel. He was unfaithful. He was dishonest. *God gave him a second chance.*

The apostle Paul had been sent to Felix. Felix was interested in hearing what Paul had to say. He listened. He heard about Jesus. *He couldn't decide what to do.*

Felix put Paul in prison because people said he was causing trouble. No one could prove it. Felix hoped Paul would bribe him. That means he wanted Paul to give him some money. That's how Felix would decide if Paul could be let out of prison. *He kept making bad decisions.*

Paul was a prisoner. One day he would be free. Felix was a leader. His decisions made him a "bad choice" prisoner.

Felix could have had an amazing adventure following Jesus. But he just couldn't seem to make good decisions.

When I make decisions, God, I will ask You for help. I don't want to make decisions on my own because they could be wrong. Will You help me?

FESTUS

As Paul was speaking for himself, Festus cried out in a loud voice, "Paul, you are crazy! All your learning keeps you from thinking right!"
ACTS 26:24

The name Festus meant "festival." But Festus did not seem festive. When Felix left, it was Festus who had to decide what to do with the apostle Paul. He had been left in prison. Festus was curious about this man who seemed to make some people very angry.

Paul came to see Festus. He told his story. King Agrippa was there and wanted to hear what Paul said too. Paul finished speaking. Festus couldn't find anything wrong with what Paul said or what he had done. But Festus would not make a decision to release Paul. Instead, Festus sent Paul to Caesar.

Caesar would make the decision.

Festus didn't see that he could have the adventure of deciding what he believed about Jesus.

I get to make many choices, Lord. I get to decide if I will follow You. I want to follow. I know this is my best choice.

GAMALIEL

*Gamaliel was a man of the religious leaders' court.
He was a proud religious law-keeper and a teacher
of the Law. He was respected by all the people.*
ACTS 5:34

.... ☆ ....

The apostle Paul learned from a Pharisee named Gamaliel. He was very smart. But very few religious leaders followed Jesus. When Jesus was alive, they wanted Him to be quiet. When He died, they thought they had silenced Him. When He rose from the dead, they wanted everyone else to be quiet. But people kept talking.

Religious leaders tried to find a way to keep people from talking about Jesus. That's when Gamaliel said, "If this teaching and work is from men, it will come to nothing. If it is from God, you will not be able to stop it. You may even find yourselves fighting against God" (Acts 5:38–39).

Gamaliel may not have known if Jesus was the Son of God, but his adventure lay in knowing that the Good News couldn't be stopped just because some people didn't believe.

*I don't want to put up roadblocks when people
need to know You, God. I want people to find
You in the way I live my life for You.*

GIDEON

The angel of the Lord showed himself to Gideon and said to him, "The Lord is with you, O powerful soldier."
JUDGES 6:12

Imagine what it would be like if someone told you that you would become the president or a king. What would it be like to hear someone call you a great sports hero or singer? Would you believe them? Would you tell them they didn't know what they were talking about?

God's messenger angel told Gideon he was a powerful soldier. What? Gideon wasn't a soldier. He was a farmer. Gideon told the angel that he didn't come from the best family. God didn't pay attention to things like that. He chose Gideon, and He would help this powerful soldier who thought he was a farmer.

When it was time for battle, Gideon led the soldiers, but God won the war. God led Gideon on an adventure he didn't think was possible. *That's the point.* God can make impossible things possible.

I want to achieve things because You help me, God. Help me dream Your dreams for my life and then choose to walk with You until I get there.

HAMAN

*When Haman saw that Mordecai did not bow
down or honor him, he was very angry.*
ESTHER 3:5

Haman worked for King Xerxes. He thought he was very important. People treated him like he was very important. He wanted people to think he was very important. There was just one problem. Another man who worked for the king did not treat him as if he was the most important. Haman wanted Mordecai to bow down to him. Mordecai believed he could not bow to anyone but God.

Haman was angry. He was frustrated. He wanted to get Mordecai in trouble. He even wanted to kill Mordecai. Haman convinced the king to make a law that would make it possible for Haman to hurt Mordecai. That's where any real adventure Haman could have had ended.

His plan failed. Mordecai was honored, and Haman's bad choices were discovered. Nothing worked out the way Haman thought it would. Anger and frustration never lead to good decisions.

*Help me be careful when I'm angry, God. I might want
to say mean things or do something to hurt others'
feelings. Help me trust You and forgive them.*

HEALED LEPER

One of them turned back when he saw he was healed.
He thanked God with a loud voice.
LUKE 17:15

·············· ☆ ··············

If you could ask Jesus for one thing, what would it be? More of something? Less of something else?

Ten men met Jesus. Each had a skin disease that kept them away from their families. They wanted to go home, but the only way they could was if they were healed. Guess what? They asked Jesus to heal them. *He did.*

Maybe they thought about their families as they began walking away. Then one man stopped. He turned around. He looked at Jesus. He thanked Jesus for his miracle.

The man was from Samaria. Samaritans didn't expect to be treated well. They were often the people who seemed to be outside looking in. But this man with a skin disease understood he had been freed to experience a new adventure. The One who freed him was Jesus.

I've been on the outside looking in, Lord. I know what
it feels like to not belong. The man with the skin
disease felt that way. So did Jesus. Thanks for
the invitation to join Your family.

HEZEKIAH

Hezekiah did what was right in the eyes of the Lord.
2 KINGS 18:3

Hezekiah was a king in Judah. Not every king was good. Not every king was bad. The Bible says, "There was no one like [Hezekiah] among all the kings of Judah before him or after him" (2 Kings 18:5).

That verse says a lot. David was a good king. Solomon was a good king. Hezekiah? *There was no one like him.* He did what was right in the eyes of God. He even made it nearly impossible to worship anyone but God. Why? Hezekiah knew there was no one like God. No one could love people like God. No one was worth serving like God.

God gave Hezekiah the adventure of making it easier for people to trust God. He was a good example to the people, and he did everything he could to encourage the people to love God and serve Him well.

I want to walk closely with You, God. I want to be a good example. I never want to make it hard for people to find You. When people look at my life, I want them to see You.

HOPHNI AND PHINEHAS

"Your two sons, Hophni and Phinehas,
will both die on the same day."
1 SAMUEL 2:34

The Pharisees looked like people who should love God. They said they loved Him. But the choices they made indicated they thought more about themselves than God. The rules they kept helped them brag about how good they were. Hophni and Phinehas weren't Pharisees, but they acted like them. Their dad was the priest Eli. They worked in God's house. They seemed to think of themselves as very important.

The problem was they had forgotten God. *God should always be remembered.* Hophni and Phinehas were bad examples of what it looks like to love God and worship Him. God wanted better role models. He expects more from people who serve Him.

These two brothers missed out on their great adventure because they didn't follow the Adventure Guide. They chose their own adventure and dishonored and disregarded God. Don't be like Hophni and Phinehas.

You gave me an example, God, so I can be an example.
Help me be an example for someone else.

HUNGRY LEPERS

Now there were four men at the city gate with a bad skin disease. They said to one another, "Why do we sit here until we die? If we go into the city, there is no food there and we will die. And if we sit here, we will die also."
2 Kings 7:3–4

People who need help sometimes do desperate things. What does that look like? The Bible shares a story of four men with leprosy. They were hungry. A war was coming. The men waited, and waited, and then waited some more. Maybe someone would feed them. When no help came, they made a decision.

They went to the city. There might not be any food. They could be killed. But they were certain that if they didn't go, they would die of hunger.

These four desperate men found food. They ate as much as they wanted and then just a little bit more. Their adventure was showing that when people have nothing else to try, they just might become brave enough to seek help.

I can be like these four desperate men, God.
Help me be brave enough to come to You for rescue.

HUR

Moses' hands became tired. So they took a stone and put it under him, and he sat on it. Then Aaron and Hur held up his hands, one on each side. His hands did not move until the sun went down.
EXODUS 17:12

Hur worked with Moses when the people of Israel wandered in the wilderness for forty years. He was a leader who had the heart of a servant. When Moses needed help, Hur helped. Once during a battle, God promised that the army would be successful as long as Moses raised his arms. Raising your arms is easy at first, but it gets harder every minute you keep them raised.

When Moses couldn't hold his arms up any longer, Hur brought a rock for him to sit on and then he helped Moses keep his arms lifted. Hur didn't wait for a better job. Hur didn't wait for an assignment he liked. Moses needed help, and that was all Hur needed to know.

Hur's adventure was seeing what needed to be done and making that his top priority.

I want to be trustworthy, God. I want You to be able to ask me to help, and I want to say, "Yes."

HUSHAI

Hushai the Archite was the king's friend.
1 CHRONICLES 27:33

Hushai served King David. He was a friend. He became a spy. When David's son Absalom tried to take the kingdom from him, Hushai joined Team Absalom. But Hushai was there to help David. He let David know what Absalom was planning. He offered advice that would not be useful to Absalom.

Hushai became a spy because King David suggested he should. The advice that Hushai gave to Absalom stopped him from taking David's throne. Hushai stopped Absalom's bad decision.

When you are a king, it can be hard to find a true friend. Hushai was called a friend of King David. He was more than a servant. More than an employee. More than a person who had good ideas. Hushai cared about David and knew that what Absalom was doing was wrong.

Hushai's adventure started a long time before he became a spy. He became friends with the man who wrote most of the psalms. He helped the king who was called a man after God's own heart.

I need to choose good friends, Lord.
Help me find them and then care deeply for them.

ISAIAH

*Before Isaiah had gone out of the center room,
the word of the Lord came to him.*
2 KINGS 20:4

.... ☆ ....

Some people thought Isaiah was really good at predicting the future. Isaiah knew better. What he did wasn't a magic act. "The word of the Lord came to him." Isaiah didn't give his opinion about what *might* happen. He gave God's promise about what *would* happen.

Isaiah was a messenger. God told him what to say, and Isaiah wrote those words. Isaiah may be best remembered for telling everyone what it would be like when Jesus came to earth. He wrote about Jesus as much as seven hundred years before Jesus was born. These are some of the words Isaiah wrote: "He took on Himself our troubles and carried our sorrows. Yet we thought of Him as being punished and hurt by God, and made to suffer" (Isaiah 53:4).

Isaiah had a faith adventure. He never saw Jesus, but he believed what God said and wrote about the way Jesus would rescue people.

*Jesus has made it possible for me to talk to You.
Your words in the Bible let You talk to
me. Help me listen, Lord.*

ISHMAEL

Hagar gave birth to Abram's son. And Abram gave his son who was born of Hagar the name Ishmael.
GENESIS 16:15

God had promised Abram a son. Ten years had passed since the promise was made, and Abram's wife, Sarai, thought that maybe God had forgotten the promise. She didn't ask God for help. She didn't ask for patience. She didn't even ask God to make things clear. Sarai thought she knew a better way. A younger woman named Hagar worked for the couple. Maybe God's promise would happen if Hagar was Abram's wife.

A boy was born to Hagar. His name was Ishmael. But Sarai and Hagar didn't get along. When Ishmael was a young man, he was sent away from Abram and Sarai. He would become the father of his own nation. His family often fought with Abram's other son, Isaac, and his family.

Ishmael lived with the poor choices that others made. His adventure was becoming the nation God promised.

Not everything I think will happen turns out the way I thought it would, God. Help me refuse to become bitter when bad things happen. Help me trust Your plan more than mine.

ISRAEL

And the man said, "Your name will no longer be Jacob, but Israel. For you have fought with God and with men, and have won."
GENESIS 32:28

.... ☆ ....

This story is another example of someone whose name was changed by God.

Here's what led to the name change: Jacob's twin brother, Esau, sent a message that he was looking for him. In fear, Jacob sent his family away. Jacob was alone when he found someone he didn't expect. Jacob wrestled with an intruder until morning. When the sky lightened, the intruder wanted to leave. Jacob wouldn't let him go. This intruder was actually God. He prayed a blessing over Jacob, changed his name to Israel, and then disappeared.

This may seem like a strange story, but one of the best words to describe what happened was that Jacob *prevailed*. That doesn't mean he beat God, but he held on just the right amount of time. God blessed him. His adventure was turning his back on what he had been and becoming a different person.

I can't fight against You and win, God. But I can hold on to You and wait for Your blessing. When You win, I win.

ISSACHAR

There were 200 captains of the sons of Issachar.
They understood the times and had much understanding of
what Israel should do. And all their brothers obeyed them.
1 CHRONICLES 12:32

⋯⋯⋯⋯⋯⋯⋯⋯ ☆ ⋯⋯⋯⋯⋯⋯⋯⋯

Issachar was one of Joseph's brothers. He would have been with his brothers when they sold Joseph as a slave. He would have been with them when they went to Egypt to buy food. He would have been sad when Joseph told his brothers who he was when they came to buy food the second time.

Issachar's family would be remembered as people who "understood the times and had much understanding of what Israel should do." This means they wouldn't make quick decisions that got them in trouble. They thought carefully about decisions and made wise choices.

Issachar's big adventure may have happened only after he made decisions he felt bad about. That's called regret. But when he learned that bad decisions hurt other people, maybe he began to learn that good decisions helped his family.

Help me understand what seems hard to understand,
God. Forgive me and help me learn from
my mistakes. I need You to teach me.

73

JABEZ

Jabez was more a man of honor than his brothers.
1 Chronicles 4:9

Jabez prayed, and some people thought he was selfish. But God didn't think so. The Bible says he was "more a man of honor than his brothers." This was his prayer: "O, if only You would bring good to me and give me more land! If only Your hand might be with me, that You would keep me from being hurt!" (1 Chronicles 4:10).

Jabez wanted good things, more land, God's blessing, and freedom from pain. There must have been a good reason for the prayer Jabez prayed. What if he wanted these things so he could bless other people?

In any case, God gave Jabez what he asked for.

Jabez's adventure was being bold, courageous, and strong. It was understanding God well enough that he could pray a prayer God wanted to answer.

May the things I ask for look like the things You want to give me, God. You always bless me. Help me accept every one of Your blessings.

JACOB

*Then Jacob made a promise. He said, "If God will
be with me and take care of me as I go. . .
then the Lord will be my God."*
GENESIS 28:20–21

.... ☆ ....

Jacob didn't start out seeking to please God. He was a deceiver. That means he wanted people to believe things that weren't true. He caused people to do things they shouldn't have done. Jacob's deception got him into trouble. It almost got him killed.

One night, as Jacob slept, God showed up in a dream. God promised Jacob land for his family. He promised always to be with Jacob. God even told him that He would keep working until the promise was delivered.

God would change the heart of a deceiver. He would change his name, future, and family.

Jacob's adventure was change. He needed to change the way he thought, acted, and treated others. He accepted the adventure of change, and it made all the difference.

*I want to be brave enough to let You change me, Lord.
Work on my heart, and then move on to what I say
and do. You can change me. Let me let You.*

JAIRUS

A man named Jairus was a leader of the Jewish place of worship. As he came to Jesus, he got down at His feet. He asked Jesus if He would come to his house.
LUKE 8:41

His daughter was dying. Jairus knew only one man could help him—Jesus. Jairus sought Him. He found Him. He asked Him to come quickly. But many other people also needed the help only Jesus could give. As each minute passed, things got worse for the little girl.

When Jesus finally arrived at the house where the girl lay, He was told she had already died. Jesus asked Jairus to believe. *Jairus believed.* Jesus went to where the girl lay and said, "Little girl, I say to you, get up!" *She got up.*

Jairus saw a miracle. He saw something that seemed impossible. He held his daughter instead of planning a funeral. This was an adventure he could share with his grandchildren. God answered his prayer.

I've never seen You raise someone from the dead, God. But I know Jesus did, and He promised a place where I can live with You forever. Let that be enough. Thank You.

JAMES

(Half brother of Jesus)

The mother of Jesus and His brothers came to Him.
They could not get near Him because of so many people.
LUKE 8:19

Three people in the New Testament are named James. Two were disciples. One wasn't. This is his story. This James was the son of Mary and the half brother of Jesus.

Jesus was the perfect example to His siblings. That doesn't mean they always liked Jesus. He didn't seem to get into trouble. *They did.* During His ministry, Jesus spoke to thousands, and many people talked about Jesus. His brothers thought He should come home.

The Bible mentions two brothers who learned to believe that Jesus came to help them meet His Father, God. James was one of those brothers. He would eventually write the book of James. This half brother would write, "I am a servant owned by God and the Lord Jesus Christ" (James 1:1).

Jesus came to rescue even His brother. James's great adventure was watching Jesus, learning from Him, and being rescued by Him.

Help me learn from Jesus, Lord. Help me remember
all He did so that I could have all of You.

JAMES

(Son of Alphaeus)

The others were Andrew, Philip, Bartholomew, Matthew,
Thomas, James the son of Alphaeus, Thaddaeus,
Simon the Canaanite, and Judas Iscariot.
MARK 3:18–19

The Bible is full of wonderful stories about people doing memorable things. David faced Goliath. Jonah faced a big fish. Jesus faced the cross. You've probably read about men of the Bible you'd never heard of before. Each had the opportunity to follow God and live for Jesus or to turn away.

Jesus had twelve disciples. There might be a few disciples you didn't know about. James the son of Alphaeus is one of those disciples. People have tried to prove that he was a cousin to Jesus. Others aren't so sure.

But the really big adventure news is that James the son of Alphaeus got to spend about three years with Jesus. He was there in all the stories the Bible mentions about Jesus interacting with and teaching His disciples. He saw what we can only read about. He heard what Jesus said. We may not know a lot about James, but James knew a lot about Jesus.

May I be known more for following You than
for anything else I do, God. Teach me.

JAMES

(Son of Zebedee)

Jesus went on a little farther. He saw James and his brother John who were sons of Zebedee. They were in a boat mending their nets.
MARK 1:19

Think really hard about what it was like to meet Jesus. James might not have expected to see Jesus at all. He was a fisherman with his brother, John, and his father, Zebedee. Maybe they fished earlier in the day and then fixed their nets. Maybe they told jokes. Maybe they talked about how the fishing had been. Maybe they wondered if they would always be fishermen. Then? Jesus came along.

Jesus called out to James and his brother. The nets would remain unmended. Their dad would be left on the boat without their help. The new stories they told would be about Jesus.

James's adventure was in being willing to have Jesus rearrange his life story. There was nothing wrong with being a fisherman. There was everything right with accepting God's new adventure.

When You ask me to go, God, help me walk in the right direction. When You tell me to stop, I don't want to take even one more step. What should I do next?

JASON

*"These men who have been making trouble
over all the world have come here also.
And Jason has taken them in."*
ACTS 17:6–7

Do you know what the word *hospitable* means? It's being kind and generous to guests and strangers. Showing hospitality means you never make someone pay for an act of kindness.

When the apostle Paul came to Thessalonica, he needed a place to stay. Paul and his friends stayed with Jason. Some people didn't like what Paul said about Jesus. They were angry with Paul. Then they got angry with Jason. They didn't think it was right for Jason to show kindness to Paul and his friends.

Jason was arrested. He nearly went to jail. But the only thing he had done was show hospitality to men who shared God's rescue plan. That's the adventure Jason is remembered for. He was kind and generous to Paul and his friends. Paul could stay and tell people about Jesus because Jason gave him a place to stay. As a result, people came to know and love Jesus.

*Being kind and generous seems like something
I could do, God. Would You help me do it?*

JEHOIADA

*Then Jehoiada made an agreement
between himself and all the people and the king,
that they should be the Lord's people.*
2 CHRONICLES 23:16

Joash wouldn't have remembered his grandmother. He was hidden from her by the priest Jehoiada. Joash was a year old when his dad, King Ahaziah, died. If Jehoiada hadn't hidden Joash, the boy also would have died.

Jehoiada learned that Joash's grandmother ordered that the royal family be killed. She wanted to be queen. For six years Jehoiada taught Joash about God. The boy needed to follow God if he was going to lead the people when he became king. Jehoiada wasn't just a priest. He was also an uncle to Joash. He might have even been thought of as a father.

Jehoiada helped Joash remember that he served God before he served the people. Jehoiada's adventure was all about teaching, training, and reminding a young king that the future was important enough that it was worth choosing to honor God.

Thank You for people who help me learn about You, God. May I follow You because they have taught me well enough that I can't help but take steps in Your direction.

JEHOSHAPHAT

*Jehoshaphat said, "Is there not another man who speaks
for the Lord here, that we may ask him?"*
1 KINGS 22:7

People remembered King Ahab, but not because he was
a good king. He didn't follow God. He found other things
to worship. He encouraged others to do the same thing.

King Jehoshaphat lived in a neighboring kingdom.
He loved and followed God. Ahab asked Jehoshaphat
to help him fight against people he called enemies. King
Jehoshaphat was willing, but he knew they should ask
God before going to war. *God had answers.*

There were men who said they spoke for God, but
Jehoshaphat wasn't convinced. He asked if there was one
more man who spoke for God. Ahab wasn't happy. He
didn't want anything standing in his way. He wanted to
fight. He wanted to win.

Jehoshaphat's big adventure was knowing whose
answer was worth listening to. He knew that God could
be trusted even when other people made bad choices.

*When I need the best answer, God, help me remember to
ask You the question. When I ask, help me trust that Your
answer is always better than anything I could come up with.*

JEHU

So Jehu got rid of Baal from Israel.
2 KINGS 10:28

God asked Jehu to do something very specific, and He commanded Jehu to stop once his job was done. But Jehu did not stop. He hurt people. He declared people guilty who were innocent. God asked Jehu to bring justice. God gave him limits. God wanted Jehu to take something wrong and make it right. But Jehu liked being judge. He wanted justice. He forgot all about mercy.

Jehu wanted other people to do the right thing, but he wasn't a good example. Jehu was pleased when other people were loving and kind, but he didn't want to be. Jehu thought he made the rules. That's why he couldn't do what God asked him to do. Jehu didn't want God to be in charge. Jehu didn't want to follow God's rules.

Jehu's adventure was supposed to be about following God, but that adventure ended when he thought he was more important than God.

I don't want to add anything to what You ask me to do, God. Help me do just what You say and then wait to discover what I should do next.

JEPHTHAH

Now Jephthah the Gileadite was a powerful soldier.
JUDGES 11:1

··························  ··························

Jephthah's brothers didn't like him very much. They even forced him to move away from them when he was old enough. He worked hard, grew strong, and became a powerful soldier.

One day his brothers came to visit. They may have been a little embarrassed. While they hadn't shown him much kindness, they now needed his help. The men of Ammon had come to Israel to fight. They said that Israel had stolen land from them years before when Moses led the people to God's promised land. Jephthah knew that God had given them the land.

Jephthah's brothers even promised to make him their family leader if he would lead the battle against the men of Ammon. God helped Jephthah to defend Israel. Jephthah fought his way through twenty cities and the matter was settled.

Jephthah could have become very bitter. He could have told his brothers to fight the battle without him. His adventure was not in joining his brothers as a soldier, but in joining God as a servant.

May I follow You, God, even when it means standing with people who don't seem to like me.

JERIMOTH

[Jerimoth was] chosen by King Hezekiah.
2 CHRONICLES 31:13

Eight different men in the Bible were named Jerimoth. The one you're reading about is found in the second "book of lists" known as 2 Chronicles. These two books are filled with the names of people. It can be easy to feel lost in these lists of names. But search long enough and you can find some great stories.

The Jerimoth in this story worked in the temple in Jerusalem. That may not seem like much, but Jerimoth worked there because he loved God. King Hezekiah chose him for the job. Why is that important? The Bible says, "There was no one like [Hezekiah] among all the kings of Judah before him or after him" (2 Kings 18:5).

A godly king picked a godly man to work in the place where God made His home.

Jerimoth's adventure may have started with the respect of King Hezekiah, but it continued every day when he made the decision to serve God with all his heart.

Every day I get the chance to serve You, God.
Help me not only want to serve You,
but serve You well in everything I do.

JETHRO

Now Moses was taking care of the flock of his
father-in-law Jethro, the religious leader of Midian.
EXODUS 3:1

Moses lived in the open country of Midian. He took care of livestock. He enjoyed a quiet life. Jethro was an older man who had a daughter named Zipporah. Moses married Zipporah. Her family became his family. Jethro would teach Moses many things. Then God called Moses to go to Egypt to rescue the people of Israel. Moses said goodbye to Jethro. He had a job to do for God.

After Moses rescued the people, Jethro made the trip to visit his family. He was proud of Moses. He worshipped God. Maybe Jethro watched his grandsons play and then noticed how hard Moses worked. Jethro thought there had to be a better way. He wanted to help Moses lead the people, but Moses needed others to help him.

Jethro's adventure was being wise. He was courageous enough to tell Moses that he couldn't keep working so hard. In the same way, God will use other people to help you become the boy He wants you to be.

You want me to be strong, courageous, and faithful.
God, help me be all three—for You.

JOAH

When they called to the king. . .Joah the son of
Asaph came out to them. . . . Joah wrote
down the things of the nation.
2 KINGS 18:18

Was Joah a newspaper writer? Not exactly. Was he a blogger? No. Did he write pretend stories? No. Joah worked for King Hezekiah and wrote about everything happening around him. He kept track of the things happening to a good king and the nation he served.

Even when bad things happened, Joah wrote about it. King Hezekiah must have been encouraged when he could read Joah's words and then see how God helped him through every struggle. Kings would sometimes ask their history writers to read some of what they wrote about an event. Joah could remind the king of the good things God had done.

Joah's adventure was using something he knew how to do to help a king remember that God is incredibly good.

I can write down the things we talk about, God. It can help
me remember what I thought and remind me of all
that You have done to show Your love to me.

87

JOASH

Joash did what was right in the eyes of the Lord all his days, because Jehoiada the religious leader taught him.
2 Kings 12:2

.... ☆ ....

Joash would be king for forty years. He was a good king—at least at the beginning.

You've read about Jehoiada. He was the man who trained Joash to be a leader who put God first in the choices he made, the things he said, and the way he cared for people. As long as Jehoiada lived, Joash led the people wisely. Joash was always learning.

When Jehoiada died, Joash stopped learning. He forgot what he had already learned. He started doing only the things he wanted to do. The people were confused. Joash had been a king who wanted God to be served and who wanted to use money dedicated to God to repair the temple. When he forgot God, he started following other gods.

Joash had two adventures. The first was following God faithfully and learning about what pleased God. His second, not-so-great adventure found him walking away from God.

There will be days when following You seems hard, Lord. Walk with me. Teach me. Help me take each step in Your direction.

JOB

There was a man in the land of Uz whose name was Job.
That man was without blame. He was right and good,
he feared God, and turned away from sin.
JOB 1:1

Job made good choices for days, weeks, months, and years. He had a big family and lots of livestock. People looked up to Job.

So when most of his family and livestock died, people decided that Job must have turned his back on God and started to make bad choices. Job knew that wasn't true. God knew that wasn't true.

Three friends made sure Job knew they thought he'd done something wrong. These friends didn't blame Job once or twice but kept blaming him day after day.

Job's wife told Job he should blame God for all the bad things that happened. She wanted him to turn his back on God. *Job wouldn't do that.*

The adventure Job experienced started in sadness, passed through frustration, and led to a close and loving relationship with the God who is completely trustworthy.

Not every day will be a perfect day, God. I might suffer.
I might not understand. Thank You for walking
with me and proving You can be trusted.

JOEL

*This is the word of the Lord that came to Joel,
the son of Pethuel.*
JOEL 1:1

.... ☆ ....

Joel was a messenger prophet. God told him what to say, and Joel made sure people heard. People didn't think God needed to send a message. The farmers had good crops. Business owners had lots of customers. People had lots of money.

When people hear that hard times are coming they might believe that if they just have enough money, they won't have any problems. God wanted the people to know that their choices were bringing the bad times. No amount of money could make these days go away. Money could not protect the people. Only God could do that.

The bad days started when locusts ate the farmers' crops—the food people ate—making it hard for people to afford things they thought would be easy to buy.

Joel's adventure was knowing what God said would happen and doing his best to make sure other people knew what God said.

*You have a lot to say about a lot of things, Lord.
Help me believe that even in bad times You can
bring good things to people who love You.*

JOHN

Jesus took with Him Peter and James and his brother John.
He led them up to a high mountain by themselves.
MATTHEW 17:1

.... ☆ ....

There were three disciples Jesus spent just a little more time with. John was one of those disciples. He was a fisherman, but a follower. He was careless, but compassionate. He was loud, but loyal.

Jesus would die soon, but before He was betrayed, He took three disciples to a mountain to pray. John followed Jesus to the place of prayer. He tried to pray but got tired. He fell asleep while Jesus prayed about what was going to happen to Him. John had said he would pray, but he couldn't. He failed Jesus, but Jesus said He still loved John. Jesus proved He was faithful to failed followers.

John made a promise he couldn't keep, but his great adventure was learning loyalty from the One who always keeps His promises. John followed Jesus for the rest of his life.

When I break a promise, God, help me remember You keep Yours. You want to forgive me. Help me learn from You and keep coming back to You every time I break Your rules.

JOHN MARK

Saul and Barnabas went back to Jerusalem after they had finished their work. They took John Mark with them.
ACTS 12:25

.... ☆ ....

Wouldn't it be nice if people never let you down? You wouldn't need to forgive anyone. You'd never have to learn to show mercy. You'd never understand how important it is for Jesus to forgive and show mercy to you.

John Mark needed forgiveness. He said he would help the apostle Paul but then left before the work was done. John Mark needed mercy. He had no good excuse and knew he had made the wrong choice.

Paul would forgive John Mark. Paul would even say that John Mark was useful to him. This is called restoration. That means to do what needs to be done to make something broken useful again.

John Mark's adventure was knowing that he needed to be forgiven and letting God change his heart. John Mark went from feeling useless to being useful.

*I want to be forgiven, God. I want to be useful.
I need mercy. I need You. Bring me back to
You every time I make the wrong choice.*

JOHN THE BAPTIST

There was a man sent from God whose name was John.
He came to tell what he knew about the Light so
that all men might believe through him.
JOHN 1:6–7

John the Baptist was sent by God. John followed where God led. He had a message to share. It was a different message than other messenger prophets shared. God wasn't telling people that He was giving them a time-out. God wanted John to tell people about His love, His Son, and His wonderful plans.

Most messenger prophets were sad because people didn't believe the message they shared. A lot of people thought John was the person they should follow. They came out to the wilderness to hear him speak. People liked John, but John knew he was supposed to help people get ready for Jesus.

John's adventure was doing exactly what God sent him to do. When his job was over, John needed to step back. He could have tried to steal the spotlight, but when Jesus came, John let God's Light shine.

Help me always remember that You are famous, God.
Help me remember that Someone famous loves me.

JONAH

*The Word of the Lord came to Jonah. . .saying,
"Get up and go to the large city of Nineveh,
and preach against it. For their sin has come
up before Me." But Jonah ran away.*
JONAH 1:1–3

Imagine God telling you to go to the school bully and say that God wanted him to stop being mean. That might be a job you wouldn't want. What if he was mean to you? Maybe you were hoping God would punish him instead.

Jonah didn't want to do what God asked him to do. He was supposed to go to Nineveh and tell the people there to stop being mean and rude and to stop breaking God's rules. They were bullies. Jonah didn't want to talk to them. He thought they should be punished.

The rest of Jonah's story involves a sea voyage, a man overboard, and a big fish with a big appetite. Jonah spent three days in the belly of that fish thinking about God's request.

Jonah's adventure didn't start with a sea voyage. It started when he chose obedience.

*When I obey You, God, I learn something
about me. I learn about others. I learn about
You. Help me obey. I have a lot to learn.*

JONATHAN

*So Jonathan told David, "My father Saul wants to
kill you. I beg you, be careful in the morning.
Stay hidden in a secret place."*
1 SAMUEL 19:2

Jonathan was the son of Israel's first king. There was no
reason to think he wouldn't be Israel's next king. Well,
there was *one* reason. The messenger prophet Samuel
said that the honor of being the next king belonged to
a shepherd who was also a soldier. That man was David.
That man was Jonathan's best friend. King Saul did not
like that man. Saul wanted to kill David.

Jonathan did something unexpected. He cared more
for his friend than the king's bad idea. He agreed with
God—*David should be king*—and knew that Saul should not
kill David. Jonathan helped his friend know when to escape.

God's plan made Jonathan's big adventure possible.
He chose friendship over fame. He chose loyalty over
royalty. Jonathan chose love over a kingdom. And each
choice was a good one because it was God approved.

*I want to be satisfied knowing that You have a good plan,
God. Let me choose loyalty, friendship, and love
over anything that puts space between what
I want and what You want for me.*

JOSEPH

Now Joseph had been taken down to Egypt. . . . Potiphar, an Egyptian leader, the head of the soldiers of Pharaoh's house, bought him from the Ishmaelites.

GENESIS 39:1

Joseph was his father's favorite. Joseph wore a special coat his dad gave him. That was before his brothers sold him as a slave. It wasn't just a bad day for Joseph. It changed his life. People lied about him. He was put in prison. He showed kindness. People forgot about him. *Yet God was with Joseph.*

Every time a bad day showed up, there was a better day to look forward to. Every forgotten promise led Joseph to the place God needed him to be.

Joseph's adventure was living through struggles and believing that God was a good God, that His plans were good plans, and that God had given him something to do that no one else could. God used Joseph to save millions of people during a time when no food would grow.

You tell me that I will struggle, and I believe it, God. You tell me You'll be with me in the struggle, and I want to believe it. Help me believe that You know where to take me.

JOSEPH, MARY'S HUSBAND

*Jacob was the father of Joseph. Joseph was the
husband of Mary. She was the mother
of Jesus Who is called the Christ.*

MATTHEW 1:16

Joseph worked with his hands. He was a hard worker. He needed to work hard because he planned to get married. His new family would need his help.

Joseph almost didn't get married. God sent an angel to let him know everything would be okay. Mary would become his wife. She would give birth to God's Son, Jesus. Joseph couldn't explain it, but he believed God's good news. Joseph got married. Mary had a baby. Jesus came to change the world and the people who live here.

A hardworking man helped raise God's Son. He taught Jesus what he did to earn a living. He gave Jesus a job for as long as He wanted it. But God sent Jesus for something more.

Joseph chose trust as his great adventure. He believed the unbelievable. He had faith in God's plan. He followed because God led.

*You are worth believing, God. Help me trust You enough
to join You in the adventure You've planned for me.*

JOSEPH OF ARIMATHEA

*When it was evening, a rich man came from the
city of Arimathea. His name was Joseph.
He was a follower of Jesus also.*
MATTHEW 27:57

Joseph of Arimathea was a religious leader who followed Jesus. No one expected that. Most religious leaders didn't like seeing people follow Jesus. They probably would have been mad if they knew Joseph wanted to learn from Jesus.

The other leaders said Jesus had broken the law. People believed what they heard. Soon people began yelling. They wanted Jesus to die. *The crowd got their way.*

It was a very sad day. Jesus was nailed to a cross. The sky grew dark. The earth quaked. Jesus died.

Joseph went to Pilate, the man in charge. Joseph asked if he could bury Jesus. Pilate gave his permission. Joseph gave Jesus his grave. Jesus didn't need it very long. He came back to life. *God did that.*

A big adventure was in store for Joseph when he let God make him a part of the biggest, greatest, most awesome story ever told.

*When I obey You, God, I get to live the story
You've always wanted for me. Help me trust—then obey.*

JOSHUA

*[Joshua said,] "If you think it is wrong to serve the Lord,
choose today whom you will serve. . . . As for me
and my family, we will serve the Lord."*
JOSHUA 24:15

God was in charge. Moses was the leader. Joshua helped Moses and believed in God. That's how it worked. It worked well.

The people of Israel left Egypt, and Moses led them through the wilderness. Soon the people would be home. They wouldn't have to live in tents. They could grow plants for food. God promised this place. When Joshua learned what he could learn from Moses, God told Joshua to be the leader. Joshua needed to be a good example.

When the people needed to be reminded of how good God had been, Joshua told the story of how God rescued them from Egypt, met their needs in the wilderness, and gave them a home.

Joshua's big adventure was being brave enough to ask the people to follow God and then leading them with God's help.

*Help me be brave enough to follow You, God.
Then help me be brave enough to ask
others to walk with me.*

JOSIAH

Josiah did what is right in the eyes of the Lord.
2 Kings 22:2

.... ☆ ....

King Joash said that the temple should be repaired. It was a good idea. But this wasn't a home improvement show. The king died without a national reveal of the finished work. The king forgot about this good idea. The work stopped.

Many years later there was a new king. His name was Josiah. He was eight years old when he became king. Later, when he was grown, he thought it was time for the temple to be restored. Men went to work. One day they found a scroll. This was a long page with writing that was rolled into a tube. No one had read these words in a very long time. They showed the scroll to the king and read to him what it said. Josiah cried.

A big adventure was waiting for King Josiah when he heard God's words instructing His people how to live. The king could have ignored the words as old and unuseful. Instead, King Josiah followed God's words and encouraged his people to obey.

There's something special about reading Your words, God.
I learn what You think so I can do what You ask.

JUDAH

Judah said to his brothers, "What do we get by killing our brother and covering his blood? Come, let us sell him to the Ishmaelites and not lay our hands on him. For he is our brother, our own flesh." And his brothers listened to him.
GENESIS 37:26–27

Judah was Joseph's older brother. He was with his brothers when they wanted to kill Joseph. Judah thought it was a better idea to sell Joseph as a slave. That decision saved Joseph's life, but it wasn't something you'd expect from a good brother.

These same brothers visited Egypt. Joseph recognized them. They didn't recognize Joseph. When it was time for the brothers to leave, Joseph kept one brother with him until they returned. Judah's brother Simeon stayed behind in Egypt until the rest of his brothers returned.

As he got older, Judah changed. His father gave him a blessing. His father liked the man he had become.

Judah's adventure was being willing to stop making bad choices and learning from his mistakes.

I don't like making choices You don't agree with, God. Help me decide to obey because You're just that important.

JUDAS ISCARIOT

Judas was the one who handed Jesus over to be killed.
MARK 3:19

Judas took care of the money for Jesus and the disciples. If they needed to buy anything, they got the money from Judas. He wasn't happy when Jesus received a special gift that wasn't cash.

Judas seemed to think that the more money he had, the more important he was. He saw so many miracles—Jesus proved to Judas that he didn't need money, but Judas wanted more money anyway.

One day men who worked in the temple told Judas that if he would help them arrest Jesus, they would give him money. Since money was what he wanted, Judas agreed to help. From that moment Judas made many bad decisions.

Judas was invited to the greatest adventure of his life, but he chose money over Jesus. He could have spent years telling people about what it was like to be with Jesus. But Judas is remembered for being greedy. He's not remembered for being loyal. His choices proved he did not want to be friends with Jesus. Judas chose the wrong adventure.

You are more important than money, God.
Help me always choose You first.

JUDAS, NOT ISCARIOT

*When they came into the city, they went up to a room on
the second floor where they stayed. The followers were
Peter and John, James and Andrew, Philip and Thomas,
Bartholomew and Matthew, James the son of Alphaeus,
Simon the Canaanite, and Judas the brother of James.*
ACTS 1:13

Some people called him Jude, Thaddaeus, or Judas. But they
made sure people understood he was not Judas Iscariot.

Jesus called him a disciple.

Like other disciples, Judas (not Iscariot) listened to
Jesus and followed Him down dusty roads and through
big cities. Judas believed Jesus was the Way, Truth, and
Life. Not much is written about this disciple, but he didn't
turn his back on Jesus.

After Jesus died, the disciples shared His willingness
to rescue people by saving them from sin. Judas shared
this good news. He shared it a lot.

This Judas lived the adventure of someone changed
by God's love. He literally walked with Jesus. Then he just
kept telling people how good God is.

*I want people to know how good You are, God.
Help me walk closely enough with You that
when I talk about You, people want to hear.*

KORAH

Now Korah the son of Izhar, the son of Kohath, the son of Levi, with Dathan and Abiram, the sons of Eliab, and On the son of Peleth, sons of Reuben, caused trouble.

NUMBERS 16:1

.... ☆ ....

Sometimes people will protest a decision made by a business or the government. A protest is when someone shows how unhappy they are or joins other people in asking for someone to change their mind.

Korah was a man who made the choice to protest. He didn't like Moses and thought he shouldn't lead the people through the wilderness. Korah thought he could do a better job than Moses. He found 249 other people who agreed with him, and they caused trouble for Moses. As a result, they found trouble for themselves.

They thought they could choose who led them. *God made the choice.* They thought they could be in charge. *Only God can be in charge.*

Korah thought his adventure was big, but his choices found him picking a fight with God. God placed Moses in charge. That was the end of Korah's adventure.

I never want to pick a fight with You, God.
Help me seek Your answers before I try mine.

LABAN

*Jacob saw that Laban did not show him
as much favor as he did before.*
GENESIS 31:2

Laban worked with animals. He owned a lot of them. He needed some help. When Jacob showed up wanting to marry Laban's daughter Rachel, Laban was certain he'd found the help he needed. Laban promised to let Jacob marry his daughter if he stayed for seven years and helped him take care of his animals. Seven years became fourteen. Fourteen years became nearly twenty.

Laban didn't want Jacob to leave, but Jacob didn't want to stay. Laban tricked Jacob. Jacob was tired of being tricked. Laban was dishonest. Jacob was tired of lies.

Laban could have had the adventure of treasuring family and wanting the best for them. The adventure he followed kept him distant from family as he thought only of himself and what he wanted. This wasn't the adventure God wants for anyone. It isn't the adventure God has for you.

*Help me remember, Lord, that You want me to enjoy
friendships and family. Help me see the people
You have given me to love as valuable gifts.
Help me encourage them to grow in You.*

LAME BEGGAR

The man who could not walk looked at them.
He thought he would get something from them.
ACTS 3:5

Jesus had risen from the dead and gone back to heaven. His closest friends became very good at telling His story. One day while they were talking to a crowd, Peter and John heard a man calling to them. He couldn't walk. He needed help. The man asked for money, but Peter and John gave him something much better.

They told him they didn't have any money, but with Jesus' help the man was healed. They took his hand, and the man who couldn't walk took his first step. What made this miracle even better was that the first place the man walked to was the temple where he could worship the God who heals.

There's always adventure when you know Jesus has changed your future. For the man who was healed, there was a great adventure in being grateful. God's gifts are often unexpected and always better than you can imagine.

I don't need to understand everything about You, Lord,
to know that You love me. Help me celebrate Your
gifts to me. Help me use them wisely.

LAZARUS

Jesus loved Martha and her sister and Lazarus.
JOHN 11:5

.... ☆ ....

It's important to remember that Jesus had friends. People have always been important to Jesus. He had friends called disciples. He has friends who follow Him today. He had friends who just wanted to spend time with Him. Mary, Martha, and Lazarus were these kinds of friends.

Lazarus was getting sicker every day. His sisters were certain that Jesus could heal him. They had no doubt. They sent a message to Jesus. They needed help. Days passed, and they wondered why Jesus didn't show up. Then? Lazarus died. Jesus didn't show up that day. He didn't show up the next day either. Four days after their brother's burial, Jesus finally arrived. Martha didn't understand. Everyone was sad.

Jesus asked that the grave of Lazarus be opened. Jesus called into the grave for His friend to come out. Lazarus got to see his friend again.

The adventure of Lazarus was knowing that Jesus loved him and could be trusted—no matter what.

May Your love change me, Lord. May I never use the word "maybe" when I think about whether You love me. Thanks for being my friend.

LAZARUS AND THE RICH MAN

There was a poor man named Lazarus who had many bad sores. He was put by the door of the rich man.
LUKE 16:20

Jesus was good at telling stories. It wasn't just because He had a good imagination. Jesus told stories to help people learn. One day Jesus told a story about a poor man named Lazarus and a rich man. Lazarus loved God but needed help. The rich man had no use for God and never thought he needed help.

Both men died. Lazarus went to be with people who loved God. The rich man could see the people who loved God, but he couldn't move from where he was to where they were. He even asked if Lazarus could come for a visit or at least go back and tell his family there was more to life than money. But God told the rich man that if people don't believe in Him when they hear the truth, then they won't believe even when they see a miracle.

Lazarus's adventure was knowing that God was bigger than his need.

Help me know You, love You, and believe in You, God. What I really need is just what You can provide.

LEMUEL

The words of Lemuel king of Massa,
which his mother taught him.
PROVERBS 31:1

The book of Proverbs is called a collection. You might collect cards, but Proverbs is a collection of wise sayings. Each verse has something good to say, and every day people read these wise words. *It helps.*

The very last chapter of Proverbs was written by a king. His name was Lemuel. He heard these words of wisdom from his mother. She taught him many things when he was a boy just about your age. Her words were wise. They became part of God's collection of wisdom.

King Lemuel honored his mother. He saw her live the things she taught. Her words teach boys to respect their moms. They teach husbands to honor their wives.

If you're looking to start a collection, try a wisdom collection. Proverbs is a perfect place to start.

King Lemuel's adventure was sharing God's wisdom. He learned it from his mom. She learned it from God.

I want to be someone who shares Your wisdom with others,
God. You are wise. Thanks for teaching others so they
can teach me. Please help me share wisdom too.

LOT

Now Lot, who went with Abram,
had flocks and cattle and tents of his own.
GENESIS 13:5

When you try something new, you might get excited. You could also be scared. Sometimes the things you don't know can make you afraid. Moving to a new town can do that. Leaving friends behind can also make you feel scared and lonely too.

Lot was Abram's nephew. When Abram followed God, Lot went with him. The only people Lot knew when they got to where God led them were his aunt and uncle.

Lot took care of animals. So did Abram. To make sure there was enough room for their animals, Abram told Lot to pick the land he wanted for his animals. This land grew enough plants for his animals to eat, but the people who lived there were very bad friends. The people made so many bad decisions that God asked Lot to leave the city before He judged it.

The adventure Lot started with Abram was hard. But Lot needed to follow God.

I've met some really great people, God.
None of them are You. Help me trust You
enough to know that Your way is perfect.

LUKE

Luke, the dear doctor, and Demas say hello.
COLOSSIANS 4:14

There are waiters who are also singers, PE teachers who draw beautiful pictures, and doctors who write books. That last example? That describes Luke. He used words to help people understand God's love story for people. He wrote the books of Luke and Acts in the Bible.

While he was a doctor, he was also a writer of history. He listened to people tell of when they met Jesus. They told what Jesus did for them. Luke loved hearing each story. Then, when the church was growing, Luke saw firsthand the things we read about Paul, Barnabas, Silas, and John Mark. Luke saw the miracles and heard the preaching.

Jesus was the best doctor ever. He is known as the Great Physician. Jesus spoke about amazing things. Jesus is called the Word. Maybe that's why Doctor Luke used words as his great adventure. He knew something about the healing power of God's Word.

Help me remember that You can take what I know how to do and use it to help others, God. You did that even before I ever knew You.

LYSIAS

Felix knew about the Christian religion. He stopped the court, saying, "When Lysias the captain comes down, I will decide about this."
ACTS 24:22

.... ☆ ....

The apostle Paul was on the move. He wasn't afraid to take the story of Jesus anywhere. But Paul had been warned. There were people who wanted to take him by force to kill him. What did Paul do? He trusted God. Then he met Claudius Lysias.

Lysias heard about the plot against Paul from Paul's nephew. Lysias was a commander. He had hundreds of soldiers waiting for him to speak. Lysias gave orders. Two hundred soldiers, seventy horsemen, and two hundred spearmen were sent to Caesarea. They were told to find Paul and take him safely to Governor Felix.

God used this Roman commander to rescue Paul. The big adventure Lysias began was in believing that Christians needed to be heard. He could have ignored Paul's nephew, but instead he sent help and made sure Paul could speak. People needed to hear about Jesus.

I want to tell people about You, God. I want to make sure other people can do the same. Help me never be ashamed of following You.

MALCHUS

Simon Peter had a sword. He took it and hit a servant who was owned by the head religious leader and cut off his right ear. The servant's name was Malchus.
JOHN 18:10

Jesus would be arrested. He knew it. Peter wasn't so sure. Jesus knew He would die on a cross and rise again from the dead. He knew it. Peter wasn't so sure. Jesus was ready to do what He needed to do to rescue mankind. Peter? He wasn't so sure.

The disciple Judas betrayed Jesus. When he showed up, Peter was sure of one thing—he wanted to protect Jesus. He didn't want anyone threatening Jesus. He used a sword and cut the ear off a man named Malchus who was a servant of one of the religious leaders. Malchus had come with his boss. He couldn't tell anyone what to do about Jesus. He just happened to be there. Jesus healed Malchus.

Malchus would live the rest of his life remembering the adventure of kindness.

Help me remember that no one has ever been as kind to me as You, Lord. Help me remember Your kindness by sharing it.

MAN BORN BLIND

As Jesus went on His way,
He saw a man who had been born blind.
JOHN 9:1

He was born blind. He'd never seen a rabbit, the ocean, or his parents. People argued about whether he'd sinned or his parents had sinned. They thought that was why he was blind. The man sat in silence. He didn't want to argue. He wanted to see. Then? He could. Jesus performed another miracle.

This man had mostly been ignored by people walking along the road. Some placed a coin or two in his cup. When they thought of him at all, they may have wondered what horrible sin caused him to be blind.

Because Jesus is God's Son, He knew the blind man, and He knew the parents. Jesus knew the man's disability was not the result of sin. But still, Jesus didn't need a reason to be kind. He didn't need a reason to heal. He just. . .did. The blind man loved Him for it. He was once blind, but then he could see. Then he kept talking about Jesus. That was his great adventure. He was changed, and he couldn't stop talking about it.

You keep changing me, God. Help me notice.
Let me say thanks. May I keep telling Your story.

MANOAH

There was a certain man of Zorah,
of the family of the Danites. His name was Manoah.
His wife was not able to have children.
JUDGES 13:2

⋯⋯⋯⋯⋯⋯⋯⋯ ☆ ⋯⋯⋯⋯⋯⋯⋯⋯

People don't always get what they want. You can probably think of things you've always wanted but never received. It happens to everyone.

Manoah wasn't wanting more dessert, a nicer camel, or even a better home. Manoah wanted a child. An angel showed up twice to let Manoah and his wife know that a child was on the way. God would use the child to do big things. First? Manoah and his wife had to believe in a good God who did good things for His people.

One man who had no reason to expect God to bless him with a child became a father. His name was Manoah. His great adventure was accepting an unexpected gift.

God gave him something he had always wanted—a son. Manoah loved the gift of a child. He loved the God who gave him the gift. The boy's name? Samson.

Help me accept Your good gifts, Lord. I may not
always expect or even recognize Your gifts,
but help me use what You give wisely.

MATTHEW

Matthew was sitting at his work gathering taxes. Jesus said to him, "Follow Me." Matthew got up and followed Jesus.

MATTHEW 9:9

Matthew followed directions. He collected taxes. That meant someone told Matthew how much tax to collect and he collected the tax.

People didn't like tax collectors very much. Some people didn't want to pay taxes. That meant it was probably hard for Matthew to find friends.

One day Matthew was doing his job when Jesus walked by. Jesus looked at him and said, "Follow Me." Matthew stopped collecting taxes and followed Jesus.

The religious leaders thought it was wrong for Jesus to have a follower whom they considered a sinner. That's the way the religious people thought of tax collectors. Jesus made it clear that He came for people like Matthew. There was a place for the outcasts with Jesus.

Matthew's great adventure was being unacceptable and then being found by Jesus. When Jesus accepted a sinner like Matthew, He showed that everyone can come to Him and find a new place called home. You can too.

Thank You for making me acceptable, God. Thanks for giving me a place to call home.

MATTHIAS

Then they drew names and the name of Matthias was
chosen. He became one with the eleven missionaries.
ACTS 1:26

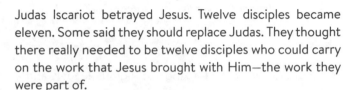

Judas Iscariot betrayed Jesus. Twelve disciples became eleven. Some said they should replace Judas. They thought there really needed to be twelve disciples who could carry on the work that Jesus brought with Him—the work they were part of.

After Jesus died, rose from the dead, and went back to heaven—but before the Holy Spirit came to help—the disciples searched for two men who were followers of Jesus when He was alive. They wanted to pick someone who loved Jesus as much as they did. They chose Matthias.

When Jesus was baptized by John, Matthias began following Jesus as a disciple. He wasn't part of the original twelve disciples. Matthias was part of a group of 120 who also followed and helped.

His adventure was continuing the journey he started with Jesus. It didn't stop when Jesus was crucified. It didn't stop when Jesus rose from the dead. His journey lasted a lifetime.

Help me remember the time that I met You, God.
Help me remember that this journey is good
and that my Trail Guide is faithful.

MELCHIZEDEK

Melchizedek's name means king of what is right. Salem means peace. So he is king of peace. Melchizedek was without a father or mother or any family. He had no beginning of life or end of life. He is a religious leader forever like the Son of God.
HEBREWS 7:2–3

Melchizedek was called a king, a religious leader, and a priest. He did what was right and lived in a place called peace. No one knew his father or mother, brother or sister. They didn't celebrate his birthday because no one knew when it was.

Some people say Melchizedek was a Christophany. That's a long word that means this king, religious leader, and priest might have been an appearance of Jesus long before He was born. Others aren't so sure.

Maybe what matters most about Melchizedek is his adventure in faithfully serving God. He followed God. He led other people. He lived in peace. He made right choices.

I want to be known as someone who follows You, God. May my choices look like choices You want me to make. Give me peace when things don't feel peaceful.

MEN OF FAITH

*Through faith we understand that the world
was made by the Word of God. Things we see
were made from what could not be seen.*

HEBREWS 11:3

The "Faith Hall of Fame." Have you ever heard of it? Maybe you've heard of the Baseball Hall of Fame. This is a place that celebrates players who did a great job. That's what the Faith Hall of Fame is all about. It celebrates people who were famous for trusting God, who believed that God was wiser than they were and that His plans were greater than their goals.

Each man on the list encountered struggles, had questions, and faced a choice. At the end of all the struggle and questions, these men chose to walk with God. They chose to trust Him, obey Him, and love Him.

You could become a man of faith. It's the adventure of a lifetime. Your name won't show up in the Bible, but God will know, and He will say, "Well done."

*I want to trust. I need to obey. Help me believe, God,
that You have the best future for me. I don't want
to believe just some of the time. Help me
make this an everyday choice.*

MEPHIBOSHETH

Mephibosheth the son of Saul's son Jonathan came to David and fell on his face to the ground in respect.
2 Samuel 9:6

Jonathan was David's best friend. When Jonathan died, King David wanted to honor his friend. He asked if there were any family members he could show kindness to. The king was introduced to Mephibosheth. He was Jonathan's son. Neither of his feet worked the way most people's feet work.

Mephibosheth needed help, and King David helped him. Mephibosheth needed food, and King David fed him. Mephibosheth needed a place to stay, and King David gave him a home.

Mephibosheth could have been bitter because David was king and not his father, Jonathan. That's what his grandfather King Saul thought would happen. Mephibosheth could have been too proud to accept King David's help. He could have been angry with the king.

The son of Jonathan found that kindness was a great adventure. Accepting David's kindness made his difficulties easier to endure. It also gave him opportunities to show the same kindness to others.

Help me not be too proud to accept the kindness of others, Lord. Help me learn to show Your kindness to those around me.

METHUSELAH

Methuselah lived 969 years, and he died.
GENESIS 5:27

It seems like every day there are new discoveries and new inventions. Ten years from now things will be very different than they are right now. People keep learning, exploring, and discovering. We like to find better ways to do things. That's just the way we are.

Methuselah lived longer than anyone else. When people live to be more than one hundred years old, we celebrate. Methuselah lived 969 years. A lot of things changed. Not all things were good. For instance, most people walked away from God.

Methuselah's father, Enoch, walked with God. Methuselah's grandson Noah walked with God. And for 969 years Methuselah saw God answer prayers, he saw God provide for his needs, he saw his family follow God, and he saw people stop honoring God.

Before Noah's big boat set sail, Methuselah ended his great adventure. He made God famous for his family. God used his family to start over after the flood.

Methuselah lived longer than anyone I know, God. Help me be a good example to my family for the rest of my life. May they recognize You in the choices I make.

MORDECAI

*But their plan became known to Mordecai and
he told Queen Esther. And Esther told the
king what Mordecai had heard.*
ESTHER 2:22

The king had lots of people who worked for him. He knew some of the people very well. There were some he had never met. There were lots of people in between. Mordecai was one of those *middle* people. He was the cousin of Queen Esther, but the king didn't know that. He followed God, but the king didn't know that. He saved the king's life, but the king didn't know that either.

One night when the king couldn't sleep, he had someone read some of the history of the country to him. That's when he heard the name Mordecai. That's when he remembered that there was a man who rescued him.

Mordecai was trustworthy. He was a hero. He saved the king. He helped save his family. His adventure was standing up for what was right even when it seemed no one noticed.

*It can be hard to make the right choice every time, God.
I need Your help. May I remember that Mordecai
made good choices because You helped him.*

MOSES

When Moses was a baby, he was hidden because the Egyptian king wanted to kill all baby boys born to Hebrew slaves. Moses was later adopted by the Egyptian king's family. That was unexpected, but it was part of God's plan to prepare Moses to rescue the people.

Moses ran away from Egypt when he was forty. When he was eighty, God was ready to send him on another great adventure. God asked Moses to go back and lead the people away from Egypt. This assignment was different than anything Moses had done before. God was making Moses into the right man to do a big job. Moses had questions. God had answers. Moses needed help. God provided miracles. Moses needed wisdom. God gave instructions.

Moses had many adventures. It's possible that his biggest adventure was learning that God could always do more than he could.

You know me completely, Lord. Help me overcome my fears. Make trusting You feel normal. Give me instructions. I want Your adventure.

NAAMAN

*Naaman the captain of the army of the king of Syria
was an important man to his king. He was much
respected, because by him the Lord had made
Syria win in battle. Naaman was a strong man
of war, but he had a bad skin disease.*

2 KINGS 5:1

Maybe Naaman thought he was going to Israel for a show. He had a skin disease. Naaman wanted to be healed. A servant girl had said there was a man in Israel who could heal him.

God used Elisha to heal Naaman. But if this was a show, Naaman didn't like it very much. Elisha didn't wave a wand or speak special words. Elisha told Naaman to go and dunk seven times in the Jordan River.

Naaman wasn't excited about it, but he walked into the Jordan River. Each time he came out of the water, his skin looked the same. Then he went down the seventh time. He was healed! It happened just like Elisha had said. As for so many others, faith was Naaman's big adventure.

*I don't have to understand why You ask me
to trust You, Lord. I just need to trust.*

NATHAN

Then the Lord sent Nathan to David.
2 SAMUEL 12:1

Sometimes God sent messenger prophets to people because the people stopped listening to Him. King David had taken something that didn't belong to him, and he wasn't talking to God about it. Maybe the king needed a good story.

God sent Nathan to talk to David. The king seemed happy to see him. Nathan told him a story about a rich farmer and a poor farmer. One had many lambs. The other had only one, and he treated it like a pet. When the rich farmer had a guest for dinner, he took the poor man's lamb and fed it to the guest.

David was very upset. He once took care of sheep. What the rich man had done was wrong. He wanted the rich man to pay for his wrong actions. Nathan simply said, "You are the man."

Nathan's adventure was delivering a hard message. It helped King David come back to God. It helped the king understand how wrong he was. It helped the king understand the importance of God's instructions.

Your instructions aren't an opinion poll, God.
What You say, You mean. Help me trust You first.

125

NATHANAEL

Philip found Nathanael and said to him, "We have found the One Moses wrote about in the Law. He is the One the early preachers wrote about. He is Jesus of Nazareth, the Son of Joseph."
JOHN 1:45

······················· ☆ ·······················

Nathanael was a skeptic. That means he needed to be convinced before he believed things. Philip had been asked to follow Jesus. He did. Philip told Nathanael about Jesus. Nathanael was from Galilee. That's where Jesus was from. He couldn't remember anyone special ever coming from Galilee. Nathanael didn't expect Jesus to be special, but then he met Jesus. He changed his mind.

Nathanael became one of Jesus' disciples. After talking with Jesus, Nathanael called Him a teacher, the Son of God, and the King of the Jews. Nathanael learned that God can use people from anywhere. He loves people from everywhere. He rescues people wherever they are.

A big adventure awaits when you become convinced that Jesus was more than a teacher, more than a king. Jesus is God's Son, and He came to rescue you.

I want to be convinced that You have a plan to rescue me, God. Trusting Jesus has always been Your answer.

126

NEBUCHADNEZZAR

Nebuchadnezzar said, "Praise be to the God of Shadrach, Meshach, and Abed-nego. . . . They changed the king's word and were ready to give up their lives instead of serving or worshiping any god except their own God."
DANIEL 3:28

Nebuchadnezzar was one of the strongest kings in the world. He made the rules, and he ignored God. Nebuchadnezzar wanted people to worship him.

This king of Babylon had dreams. God helped him understand them, but Nebuchadnezzar seemed to forget who helped him. He thought he was more important than God.

One day Nebuchadnezzar had another dream. God helped his adviser, Daniel, understand what it meant. Until Nebuchadnezzar honored God, he would wander with wild animals and eat grass for food. It would take the king seven years to finally honor God. When those years were over, King Nebuchadnezzar said, "I. . .praise and honor the King of heaven. For all His works are true and His ways are right. And He is able to bring down those who walk in pride" (Daniel 4:37).

I want to honor You in the things I say and do, God. Let my mouth be quick to say You're awesome.

NEHEMIAH

These are the words of Nehemiah the son of Hacaliah. . . .
While I was in the king's house in Susa. . .
NEHEMIAH 1:1

·········· ☆ ··········

Nehemiah wasn't home, and he knew it. Home was Jerusalem, and he was in Susa. He worked for a king who had taken the people of his country as prisoners. Nehemiah had no choice. He had to work for the king even when he wanted to go home.

Nehemiah got news from home. His brother Hanani told him that people who had come back home found that the walls around the city were broken. The gates that helped protect the city had been burned. *God's people in Jerusalem needed help.*

When Nehemiah told the king about how sad he felt, the king sent him to Jerusalem. In less than two months Nehemiah found people who would help him rebuild the walls. God was preparing the city for the return of His people. They wanted to come home.

Nehemiah's adventure was knowing that something needed to be done and then doing whatever he could to help. This is what initiative looks like.

Help me pay attention to what needs to be done
around me, God. May I help when help is needed.

NICODEMUS

There was a man named Nicodemus.
He was a proud religious law-keeper and a leader
of the Jews. He came to Jesus at night.
JOHN 3:1–2

.... ☆ ....

Nicodemus wanted to know more about Jesus. He was curious. He was willing to learn. He also knew that his friends wouldn't approve. His friends were called Pharisees, and they were sure that Jesus couldn't teach them anything. They were the ones who would try to find a reason to crucify Him. But one night the Pharisee Nicodemus came alone to see Jesus and ask questions.

While Jesus spoke to Nicodemus, He said something that was very important—God loved the people on earth so much that He made the choice to send His Son to rescue people. That meant Nicodemus. It means you. It meant then. It means today. It meant hope. It still does.

The words Jesus spoke to Nicodemus set him on a great journey. He was told that whoever trusts Jesus finds freedom. Being a Pharisee did not bring freedom. Jesus gave Nicodemus a better choice to consider.

Thanks for giving me things to think about, Lord.
Help me look for freedom in Jesus.

NIMROD

*Cush became the father of Nimrod, who was the first
on earth to become a powerful man.*
GENESIS 10:8

.... ☆ ....

Nimrod was Noah's great-grandson. He lived after the big flood. He was very strong. It was easy for some people to think of him as a leader.

He probably heard the stories of how God saved his family from the worst flood the world would ever know. But Nimrod hadn't seen the water. He didn't live with the animals inside the big boat for months. Nimrod had great role models, but he was strong. He thought he didn't need God.

Some believe that Nimrod encouraged people to work on what the Bible calls the "Tower of Babel." The people believed they could build a tower that would reach to heaven. God stopped this very bad idea. God was stronger.

Nimrod could have chosen an adventure that allowed God to use his strength to help people. But he chose pride instead of the humility that comes from knowing that God has always been most important.

*Help me see that everything I am able to do well is Your
gift to me, God. Help me do my best for You.*

NOAH

Noah found favor in the eyes of the Lord.
GENESIS 6:8

··· ☆ ·································

People broke God's law. No one was sorry. Well, there was one. Noah believed that following God *was* his big adventure. God noticed.

God told Noah to build a big boat called an ark. This boat was big enough to hold two of every kind of animal. What God asked Noah to do didn't make sense. He didn't live near water, and he'd never built a boat.

Noah worked on the ark longer than most people live. God brought the animals to Noah. People laughed at Noah when he invited them to come on board the boat. When everyone turned down the chance to be saved, God closed the door. Rain fell. Floodwaters covered the earth. Noah and his family were safe inside the ark.

Noah could have ignored God, but that wasn't the adventure he chose. He worked hard to get things ready. In the end, God did the rescuing even when there were only eight people who wanted to be rescued.

Help me remember that no matter how hard I work,
You are always the Rescuer, God. Help me trust
that You can, You will, and You have.

NUN

"Joshua the son of Nun, who stands in front of you, will go in there. Tell him to be strong, for he will bring Israel into their new land."

DEUTERONOMY 1:38

You probably recognized the name Joshua. What about the name Nun? When Joshua is mentioned in the Bible, he is often referred to as the "son of Nun."

What do we know about Joshua's dad? He was born and raised a Hebrew slave in Egypt. He saw the bad things that happened before Moses led the people toward their future.

He was probably alive when God sent birds and manna for people to eat. He might have been standing nearby when God sent water through a rock when the people were thirsty.

Nun raised a good son. People who make good choices often have parents who made good choices. Not always, but everyone needs a good example of how to live a life for God.

Nun may have been recognized for the adventure of raising a son who loved God and followed Him all the way to the land God had promised.

Thanks for good role models, God.
Help me find one. Help me be one.

OBADIAH

Ahab called Obadiah who was the boss over his house.
(Now Obadiah had much fear of the Lord.)
1 Kings 18:3

Obadiah was a good man who served a bad king. When Elijah was hiding during the three and a half years without rain, Obadiah worked for the wicked King Ahab. But Obadiah served God.

When Queen Jezebel tried to kill all of God's messenger prophets, Obadiah hid one hundred of them so they would not die. When the king wanted to find plants for his animals to eat, he sent Obadiah. On that trip Elijah found Obadiah and told him to let the king know he wanted to see him.

Obadiah was nervous. It seemed that when Elijah didn't want to be found, no one could find him. If he told the king about seeing Elijah, then he could be in big trouble if Elijah didn't show up. Elijah promised he would, and he did.

Obadiah's big adventure was knowing that no matter the name of his boss, he always worked for God.

I want to serve You even when I work for someone else, God. I want my choices to please You.

OBED

Boaz was the father of Obed.
RUTH 4:21

Ruth is a famous woman in the Bible. She was born and raised in Moab. She married a Hebrew man, but he died. Ruth followed her mother-in-law, Naomi, to Bethlehem. It was there that she met and married a farmer named Boaz.

There's a lot more to the story, but let's talk about Obed. That's what Boaz and Ruth named their son. Ruth lived through a lot of sad news. Sometimes she struggled to find enough food to eat, but God brought Boaz. Together they welcomed Obed. This boy would become the father of Jesse. Jesse would become the father of David. David would become the king of Israel. David was also an ancestor of Jesus.

Obed's adventure was probably something he didn't realize he was on. He was part of God's plan to be a relative to Israel's most remembered kings. Obed was King David's grandfather. Maybe Obed taught David how to lead sheep.

You can turn bad things into good things, God. Help me remember the story of Obed when I can't figure out why I'm living through hard days.

ONESIMUS

[Onesimus] has become my son in the Christian life while I have been here in prison.
PHILEMON 1:10

.... ☆ ....

Onesimus was a thief. That was before he was introduced to Jesus. Then? He knew he was wrong. The apostle Paul was the one who told Onesimus about Jesus.

Onesimus was more than a thief. He was a servant, but not just any servant. He was a servant who ran away from his boss, Philemon. He needed to make things right, but Onesimus wasn't sure he wanted to go back to his old boss. He knew he was in trouble. Facing his boss would be humiliating. Besides, he had taken what wasn't his.

Paul sent a letter to Philemon. Paul had introduced *him* to Jesus too. Onesimus had changed, and Paul wrote that he would consider it a personal favor if Philemon would show kindness to Onesimus.

This is the adventure of a thief who changed direction when he met Jesus. Onesimus wanted to do the right thing. His new adventure started the moment he began his walk with Jesus.

You change me from the inside when I choose You, God. Help me choose You. Help me choose to follow You every day.

PARALYTIC

*Four men came to Jesus carrying a man
who could not move his body.*
MARK 2:3

Jesus was in the house. There was no more room. Jesus spoke wise words. People outside could not hear. Jesus could heal too. Four men had a friend who needed that kind of help. They carried their friend on a sleeping mat. They wanted him to meet Jesus. But there were too many people. There seemed to be no way to bring the man to Jesus.

Then they had another idea. They carried the sick man to the roof. While he rested, the four men cut a hole in the roof above where Jesus was speaking. They attached ropes to the mat and lowered him through the roof to Jesus.

That day a sick man received two gifts. First, Jesus forgave him. Then Jesus healed him. Four men watched from the roof.

The man whose body seemed broken had some great friends, but his adventure really began the moment he walked home forgiven.

*Thank You for showing that forgiveness is more
valuable than healing, God. I have always
needed what only You can offer.*

PAUL

Then Paul stood up on Mars' Hill and said, "Men of Athens, I see how very religious you are in every way."
ACTS 17:22

Mars' Hill was a place where people talked. They loved to talk. Most thought anything could be a god. They liked to hear things they had never heard of before. So some people made things up.

Paul wanted to talk about Jesus. When he visited Mars' Hill, he found a statue dedicated to the "Unknown God." The people didn't want to leave any god out. Paul told the people that he knew who this unknown god was. Everyone gathered around Paul as he told them about Jesus. Some people laughed at him. Some people wanted to know more.

Paul didn't always believe in Jesus. At one time in his life, he may have wanted to laugh at Christians too. But Jesus changed Paul. He also changed some of the people on Mars' Hill.

It took awhile, but Paul learned that his greatest adventure would always be Jesus.

I want Jesus to be my great adventure too, God. I want to help other people understand who Jesus is and what He did for all of us. You can give me the words.

PETER

Peter said to Jesus, "If it is You, Lord,
tell me to come to You on the water."
MATTHEW 14:28

Gravity holds your feet to the ground. It keeps you from floating away. God made it. It's good. Gravity can also be tricky. . .it makes your feet sink in water, which makes it harder to cross a river. You need a bridge for that.

One day Jesus did something no one expected. He didn't sink when He put His feet in water. *Amazing.* His disciples were in a boat, and they saw Him walking on the water. Peter was one of those disciples. He asked if he could walk on water too. Jesus said he could. When Peter stepped into the water, he stayed on top. He started walking to Jesus. Peter trusted Jesus. Then he wondered how this was possible, and he began to sink.

Peter was excited for new adventures. *He wasn't always prepared.* He wanted to believe. *He didn't always trust.* He said yes. *He often changed his mind.*

Jesus still helped Peter just like He helps you.

I'd like to say I will never let You down, God,
but I will. Thanks for being willing to help me.

PHARAOH

So [the Egyptians] put men in power over [the Hebrew people] to make them work hard. And they built the store-cities. . .for Pharaoh the king.
EXODUS 1:11

The Hebrew people moved to Egypt during the worst famine anyone could remember. Nothing would grow. The people were welcome. They were guests.

But by the time Moses was sent by God to rescue the people, they were thought of as slaves. They couldn't leave if they wanted. The people of Egypt were unkind to them.

The pharaoh of Egypt was like a king. He made the rules. He didn't like the idea of letting the Hebrew slaves leave. But that's what God wanted. Ten different times God brought trouble to Egypt to help Pharaoh understand that the people needed to leave. The first nine times Pharaoh chose to refuse God. He was stubborn. He made things worse for his people. But after the tenth trouble, he let the Hebrew people go.

Pharaoh could have cooperated with God. His adventure would be remembered for kindness. Instead, this pharaoh is remembered for a foolish adventure—fighting against God.

I can't stop You from doing what You know needs to be done, God. Help me work with You—not against You.

PHARAOH'S CHIEF BAKER

*Some time later, the man who carried the king's cup
and the man who made the king's bread
did wrong against the king of Egypt.*
GENESIS 40:1

························· ☆ ·························

Joseph was in prison. He didn't deserve to be there, but when the sun went down Joseph had to sleep in prison. That's where he would start the next day—and the one after that.

Two men who worked for Pharaoh had been sent to the same prison. One baked bread. One made sure the king was refreshed. They watched Joseph. He was trustworthy. Even those in charge of the prison trusted Joseph.

When the two men who worked for Pharaoh had dreams on the same night, they thought Joseph could help them. It must have been awkward for Joseph, because one dream meant the cupbearer could go back to work. The baker? He would not.

The Bible doesn't say what bad thing the baker had done, but it was a choice. The baker had a good job, but he chose an adventure that did not look like obedience.

*Help me be trustworthy, God.
Help me learn how to do that from You.*

PHILEMON

*[Philemon,] you are a much-loved
workman together with us.*
PHILEMON 1:1

Philemon lived in Colossae. He was a leader in the church there. Paul wrote the book of Colossians to that church. He also wrote a letter to Philemon. Paul had a message Philemon needed to read.

You've read the story of Onesimus. He worked for Philemon and then ran away from him. Eventually Onesimus wanted to make things right with Philemon.

Paul had become friends with both men. He knew both before they met Jesus and after they followed Him. Philemon only knew Onesimus before he met Jesus, and he was unhappy with him.

Paul helped bring an employee and his boss together. The thing they now had in common was Jesus. Philemon needed to forgive. Onesimus needed to be restored.

A boss had the adventure of helping an employee find a way to return to work. Philemon could have stayed angry and refused to let Onesimus come back to work. Paul asked him to give Onesimus another chance. Philemon agreed.

*Please use me to help others, God. Sometimes that's
just what they need. That's what friends do.
That's what You do for me.*

PHILIP

An angel of the Lord spoke to Philip saying, "Get up and go south. Take the road that goes down from Jerusalem to the country of Gaza. It goes through the desert."
ACTS 8:26

One time Jesus asked Philip where he could buy bread to feed thousands of people. Philip reminded Jesus that they didn't have enough money to buy that much food. Jesus knew what would happen. Philip would see a miracle. A young boy's meal fed everyone.

That was one of the adventures the disciple Philip had because he followed Jesus. He also saw other miracles. God even used him to perform miracles.

Once, an angel told him to go and meet someone. That someone was a man who worked for the queen of Ethiopia. God wanted Philip to help this man understand how God could rescue him. That man accepted God's rescue. He could then take the same message back to his queen.

Philip didn't always have the answers, but he knew that God did. Philip was useful because he was willing to be used by God. That's a bold adventure.

If You want to use me, God, make me willing.
When You ask me to go, help me follow directions.

PHILIPPIAN JAILER

The man who watched the prison woke up.
He saw the prison doors wide open and
thought the men in prison had gotten away.
ACTS 16:27

He was in charge of the prison in Philippi. No one left without his permission. If they escaped, he would be in trouble. Not everyone in his jail was mean or rude, but until he was told to let them go, every prisoner had to stay put.

The apostle Paul and his friend Silas were in jail. They did something unusual. They sang songs. Each song thanked God. No one expected that. No one expected an earthquake either, but that's what happened. When the earth rumbled, the jail cells opened. Everyone could have run away. No one did.

The Philippian jailer had questions. Paul and Silas told him about the new life he could have if he followed Jesus. The jailer chose his own adventure with Jesus. It was a journey his entire family took.

I should never be surprised when someone makes the choice to walk with You, God. Their stories encourage me to take new steps with You. Thanks for this adventurous journey.

PILATE

They tied [Jesus] and took Him away. Then they handed Him over to Pilate who was the leader of the country.
MATTHEW 27:2

Pilate was a powerful man. He could lead, command, and judge. One day he was asked to be a judge. Pilate didn't want that job.

A crowd brought Jesus to him. Pilate learned that Jesus was a teacher, that the religious leaders didn't like Him, and that the people wouldn't leave him alone until he said Jesus was guilty.

Pilate didn't want to do that. He didn't believe Jesus had done anything wrong. But there was a crowd. That crowd was angry. They kept saying two words: "Crucify Him!"

The crowd's insistence made things very hard for Pilate. He liked things to be calm and peaceful, but they weren't.

Pilate wanted to let Jesus go. That would have been a great adventure. But Jesus had come to rescue people from their sin. Pilate could not save Jesus from something He *had* to do for you. Jesus died. He rose again. *Mission accomplished.*

I'm so thankful that Jesus died for my sin and lives to help me today, God. No one could be right with You without what Jesus did.

POOR BUT WISE MAN

*But a poor wise man was found in the city,
and he brought the city out of its trouble by his
wisdom. Yet no one remembered that poor man.*
ECCLESIASTES 9:15

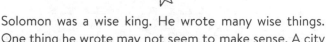

Solomon was a wise king. He wrote many wise things. One thing he wrote may not seem to make sense. A city needed a hero. A poor man who was also wise stepped up to help. The city was saved, but the man was forgotten.

No parade. No plaque to hang on the wall. No street renamed for this man. Just this one verse talks about his great adventure, but there's more to the story.

This man just might have been wise enough to help save the city without saying, "Hey, look at me." Wisdom knows that being humble is better than being boastful and proud. This man didn't need awards to do the right thing. He saved a city and went home. God knew. This man could be happy knowing that God used him to help. He knew that wisdom comes from God.

*I want to be willing to help even when no one
notices or remembers, God. Help me do
the right thing knowing that You know.*

POTIPHAR

*Now Joseph had been taken down to Egypt by
the Ishmaelites. And Potiphar, an Egyptian leader,
the head of the soldiers of Pharaoh's house,
bought him from the Ishmaelites.*

GENESIS 39:1

Slavery isn't a good idea. There was a time when people bought and sold other people. It has happened all over the world and over a very long period of time.

The Bible tells a story of an Egyptian leader named Potiphar who bought a slave named Joseph. You've read his story earlier in this book. Joseph was sold by his brothers to traders headed to Egypt. The traders sold Joseph to Potiphar. Potiphar wanted Joseph to help him in his house.

Joseph worked hard. Potiphar trusted him with everything. But that was before Potiphar's wife lied about Joseph. She told her husband that Joseph had done something wrong. Potiphar was very angry. He sent Joseph to prison, but you already know that God wasn't finished with Joseph.

Potiphar's adventure included making a decision quickly without knowing the truth. People do that today too. It always means that mistakes are made.

*Help me seek truth, God.
My feelings can lie to me. Your truth never will.*

PRODIGAL SON

"The [prodigal] son got up and went to his father. While he was yet a long way off, his father saw him. The father was full of loving-pity for him. He ran and threw his arms around him and kissed him."
Luke 15:20

································· ☆ ·································

Once a man had two sons. The older son worked hard. The younger son just wanted enough money to start a life in the city.

His dad sadly gave his younger son what he asked for. His son walked away.

Now he had money. His friends wanted him to spend it. *He spent.* Then his money ran out. *So did his friends.*

He had no place to stay, no food, and no friends. The only job he could find was feeding pigs. The pigs ate better than he did. *It was time to go home.*

The prodigal son spent everything his dad gave him, but his great adventure was discovering that his dad still loved him. The son who made the wrong choice was welcomed home.

Help me remember that even when I make mistakes You still love me, God. Help me come back to You whenever I wander away.

RABSHAKEH

*Then Rabshakeh stood and called out with a loud voice
in the language of Judah, saying, "Hear the
word of the great king of Assyria."*
2 Kings 18:28

Rabshakeh stood before God's people in Judah. He had a job to do. He told the people that the king of Assyria was on the way. They would soon be prisoners because his king would win.

The words Rabshakeh spoke made people afraid. Rabshakeh gave his message in the language spoken in Judah. Rabshakeh wanted to make sure everyone could understand his message. The people were very worried.

But Rabshakeh went too far when he said, "Has any one of the gods of the nations saved his land from the power of the king of Assyria?" (2 Kings 18:33).

King Hezekiah knew God was more powerful. This king trusted God, and God saved the people.

Rabshakeh's adventure never got started. He put his trust in the wrong things. He trusted humans, the military, and personal strength. He had no trust in the God who proved to be stronger and wiser.

*Help me trust Your strength, God. Help me believe
Your wise words. I never want to forget.*

REHOBOAM

Solomon died and was buried in the city of his father David. His son Rehoboam ruled in his place.
1 KINGS 11:43

⋯⋯⋯⋯⋯⋯⋯⋯ ☆ ⋯⋯⋯⋯⋯⋯⋯⋯

It must have been hard to be the son of King Solomon. No king was wiser.

When Rehoboam became king, he probably was tired of being compared to his dad. People wondered if he would be as wise.

Some people told the king they had too much work. They didn't want to work so hard. Rehoboam asked them to come back in a few days for his reply. The men who had worked with King Solomon suggested he make things easier on these workers. The people would appreciate it and accept him as king. But Rehoboam's friends thought he should give them even more work to do.

Rehoboam didn't ask God for help. He made things harder for the people. The people were angry. They didn't want Solomon's son to be king.

Rehoboam started his adventure as a new king but made choices that discouraged people from following him. He should have asked God for help.

Why is it so easy to try to make decisions without asking You first, God? Give me the wisdom to ask.

REUBEN

Reuben then said, "Do not put [Joseph] to death.
Throw him into this hole here in the desert.
But do not lay a hand on him." He wanted to be
able to save Joseph and return him to his father.
GENESIS 37:22

Reuben was one of the twelve sons of Jacob. He was there the day Joseph was sold as a slave. Things didn't go the way Reuben thought. The brothers decided to put Joseph in a well until they figured out what to do with him. Reuben knew his brothers were angry. He planned to rescue Joseph from the well and take him home.

When he came to get Joseph, his brothers had already sold him as a slave. He had meant to do the right thing. That would have been a great adventure he could share. Then Reuben made another decision. He could have been honest with his father. Instead, Reuben let his dad believe a wild animal had killed Joseph.

This adventure was never approved by God, and it would be a burden that Reuben carried for years.

I want to be honest even when it's hard, Lord.
I don't want to hide behind lies.

RICH YOUNG RULER

When the man heard these words, he was sad.
He walked away with sorrow because he
had many riches here on earth.
MARK 10:22

.... ☆ ....

Some people are good at following rules. That's a good thing, because rules, regulations, and laws can help people know what to do and what to avoid. The rich young ruler was a good rule follower. When he asked Jesus what he needed to do to have a life that lasted forever, Jesus told him to be faithful, never kill anyone, never steal, never lie, and always honor his parents.

Following these rules was easy for this man—he'd been doing it since he was a boy. The man asked if there was anything else. Jesus told him to sell what he had and give the money to anyone who needed it. This man admired God, but he worshipped money.

His adventure was not necessarily being poor but remembering that God is more important than money. He didn't think that was true. His adventure stopped when he walked away.

I need to remember that nothing is more important than You, God. Help me make You important.

RUFUS AND ALEXANDER

They came to a man called Simon who was coming from the country of Cyrene. He was the father of Alexander and Rufus.
MARK 15:21

Two young brothers were visiting a big city. Rufus and Alexander probably didn't know anyone. They had just arrived in Jerusalem. Their dad, Simon, had been grabbed by a Roman soldier and forced to carry the cross of a man who struggled with the burden. He had been hurt. The boys could see He was weak. It didn't take long for them to lose sight of their dad. They listened to the commotion of the people around them. Some were crying. Some were shouting. The boys wanted their dad. They probably felt frightened. They probably wanted to hold their dad's hand. But he wasn't there.

Beyond the crowd, their dad helped carry Jesus' cross to a hill called Golgotha. Rufus and Alexander would remember this adventure for a very long time. Many believe the two brothers went on to follow Jesus as adults and share His story.

I experience adventure every time I join You, God. Help me take what I learn and use it to serve You.

SAMSON

*Then the woman gave birth to a son and
named him Samson. The child grew up
and the Lord brought good to him.*
JUDGES 13:24

Samson was stronger than any other man. *God made him
strong.* Samson's long hair was connected to his strength.
He was set apart to serve God. There were foods he couldn't
eat, beverages he couldn't drink, and hair he couldn't cut.

Samson was strong because he obeyed the instructions God gave him. He defeated enemies, helped his
people, and thought he was pretty special.

When Samson thought more of himself and less of
God, he started making bad decisions. He spent time with
the wrong people and trusted the wrong girl. Samson
told a beautiful girl who did not love God about how he
had obeyed God by never cutting his hair. When Samson
took a nap, he got his first haircut. When he woke up, he
was weak—his strength had left him.

Samson's adventure involved always needing God.
His adventure took a break when he decided he could
handle things on his own.

*I can never do what You can do, God.
Help me honor Your strength by trusting Your strength.*

SAMUEL

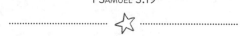

*Samuel grew. And the Lord was with him
and made everything he said come true.*
1 SAMUEL 3:19

⋯⋯⋯⋯⋯⋯⋯⋯⋯⋯ ☆ ⋯⋯⋯⋯⋯⋯⋯⋯⋯⋯

You're probably growing up in a neighborhood. Maybe you've ridden a bike, played ball, or spent time in the backyard. Things were different for Samuel. He grew up in the tabernacle, a church-like setting. That's where he learned about God. That's where he learned to speak for God.

Samuel was a messenger prophet. He needed to say the words God wanted him to say. He needed to do the things God wanted him to do. He needed to think the thoughts God wanted him to think.

God told Samuel who should be king. God even asked him to lead a battle. This messenger prophet also gave advice to kings. Samuel knew some of God's plans before anyone else. Truth was his adventure. He learned truth from God. He shared truth with everyone who needed to know it. Samuel didn't make things up. He spoke for God, trusted God, and wanted God's best for the people he served.

I may never be exactly like Samuel, God. But I want to be faithful in learning Your way so I can share Your truth.

SANBALLAT

*When Sanballat heard that we were building the wall again,
he became very angry. He was filled with anger
and he made fun of the Jews.*
NEHEMIAH 4:1

Sanballat was an angry man. *Very angry.* Almost every time he shows up in the Bible, he's upset about something. Usually he was upset about Nehemiah rebuilding the wall in Jerusalem. He was angry enough that he spent most of his time trying to stop construction.

He laughed at the people who were rebuilding the wall. He made fun of them. He tried to make them feel bad for doing a good thing. Sanballat even tried to invite Nehemiah to a meeting so he would be distracted. Nehemiah continued to work, which, of course, made Sanballat angry. *Very angry.*

Imagine what a wonderful adventure Sanballat could have had if he had been helpful instead of angry, friendly instead of scornful, and an encourager instead of a discourager. His adventure in anger did not help anyone.

*When I get angry, I don't think right. God, You can
help me discover joy instead of anger, and hope
instead of despair. It's what I need.*

SAUL

*When Samuel saw Saul, the Lord said to him,
"Here is the man I told you about. He is
the one who will rule over My people."*
1 SAMUEL 9:17

Israel had never had a king before. God knew they didn't need one. *He was their king.* His rules were right. His decisions were just. His love was for everyone. But the people wanted a human king. They wanted to be like every other nation.

God warned them that a king would do things the people wouldn't like. *They still wanted a king.* So God sent Samuel to choose a king. His name was Saul. He didn't think he was worthy. He wasn't sure he wanted the job. He even tried to hide. *Then Saul became king.*

He liked the way people treated him. He liked being powerful. He became nervous and angry if people liked anyone else better.

Saul was offered an important adventure, but he became jealous. He had everything a leader would need, but he gave it all up to chase enemies who weren't really enemies.

Help me never turn my adventure into something You didn't want it to be, God. You lead. I'll follow.

SAUL OF TARSUS

Saul was making it very hard for the church. He went into every house of the followers of Jesus and took men and women and put them in prison.

<small>ACTS 8:3</small>

.... ☆ ....

Saul grew up learning a lot about God. He went to special classes to learn more. He was a good student.

When he became a man, he heard about Jesus. People said He was the Messiah—the One everyone had been waiting for. Others said He was God's Son. Saul didn't believe it. He thought it was wrong to think that Jesus was someone special.

Saul watched when a crowd killed a follower of Jesus. He held people's coats while they punished Christians. He looked for Christians so he could put them in prison. Saul thought he was on an adventure that pleased God. Then? Jesus showed up.

No one thought Saul would follow Jesus. People found it hard to believe when they heard that he became a Christian. This was a much better adventure. Jesus changed Saul's name to Paul and made him a missionary. God can use anyone.

Even if I've made bad choices, You can still make me useful, God. I want the adventure that comes from following You.

SETH

Seth was the son of Adam.
LUKE 3:38

Seth had brothers, but he didn't grow up around them. His brother Cain killed his brother Abel. They were both full-grown men before Seth was born. He was the third son of the first man and woman, Adam and Eve.

Cain was sent away because he had killed his brother, so Seth had to learn to play by himself, explore by himself, and spend time with his parents by himself. But Seth became an older brother.

The Bible doesn't talk much about Seth. You've read about some of his relatives, like Enoch, Methuselah, and Noah. Some of the men who followed God most closely were from Seth's family.

Adam may have told Seth stories of naming animals and talking with God. Seth probably heard about the Garden of Eden and a talking serpent.

Seth's adventure was being willing to take everything he could learn about God and share it with his children, grandchildren, and even more generations of family members.

I want to grow up and tell my family about all the things I've learned about You, God. And maybe they will learn even more—so they can share even more.

SHADRACH

*Then Nebuchadnezzar became very angry and
called for Shadrach, Meshach, and Abed-nego.
And they were brought to the king.*
DANIEL 3:13

The king had a plan. It wasn't a good plan, but *he* liked it. He had a gold statue made. He wanted people to think of the statue as something to worship. *But it wasn't.* Shadrach knew it wasn't. When the king said people should honor the statue, Shadrach knew he couldn't. People knew that when special music played, everyone was expected to bow. *He didn't.* Neither did his friends. The king wasn't happy.

When the king found out that Shadrach and his friends wouldn't worship his statue, he turned a furnace into a prison. He made it very hot. Shadrach and his friends should have died when they were thrown into the furnace, but God showed up and saved them.

It's an adventure to stand up and say, "This is wrong." It's not easy, but the right words spoken at the right time change endings.

*Help me never be ashamed to say that You saved me, Lord.
You rescued me, and I worship You. You loved me,
and I can't help talking about You.*

SHEM, HAM, AND JAPHETH

On the very same day Noah and his sons, Shem and Ham and Japheth, and Noah's wife and the three wives of his sons with them, all went into the large boat.
GENESIS 7:13

They couldn't remember a time when their dad wasn't working on God's big boat. They were brothers, and they knew what their dad was building. They knew why he was building it. The boat would be their home during the worst flood in history.

Shem, Ham, and Japheth agreed to follow their dad. Noah agreed to follow God. He was on an adventure that God designed. It was an adventure that kept his family safe. But they wouldn't have been safe if they didn't do what God asked them to do.

God's big boat was filled with animals and birds, Noah and his wife, and these brothers and their wives. God was willing to rescue everyone, but only eight people accepted His gift. You're here because Shem, Ham, and Japheth were adventurers. It was God's big idea.

Letting You rescue me is just what You wanted, God. It's just what I needed. It's just what You offer.

SHEPHERDS

In the same country there were shepherds in the fields.
They were watching their flocks of sheep at night.
LUKE 2:8

Shepherds didn't hang out with a lot of other people. They spent their time with sheep. Lots of sheep. Sheep that listened. Sheep that ran away. *Sheep.*

Shepherds lived under the stars, listened for animals that wanted to eat sheep, and helped animals that never seemed to show gratitude. Most people didn't want to be a shepherd.

Then one night some shepherds were invited to spend time with three people in the nearby town. They didn't know Joseph or Mary, but when an angel said it was time to go, they didn't ask a lot of questions. They hurried into Bethlehem and met the baby Jesus.

They could have thanked the angel then explained why their job was more important. Instead, the shepherds took the time to meet the baby who would one day be called the Good Shepherd. This was an adventure in willingness. Meeting Jesus was an amazing honor—and shepherds were the very first.

Help me be willing to meet You, Lord.
It's an honor to join Your story and go where You lead.

SILAS

[Silas] preached to the Christians and helped them to become stronger in the faith.
Acts 15:32

.... ☆ ....

Just because the Bible doesn't talk about Silas as much as others doesn't mean he wasn't important. He was a missionary partner of Paul's. He was beaten and placed in prison. But Silas "preached to the Christians and helped them to become stronger in the faith."

Silas wanted people to learn about Jesus for the first time, but he also wanted Christians to see their own faith grow. He wanted to see Christians act like Jesus. He didn't want them to make guesses about what they should do.

Silas knew that Christians who really followed Jesus had the best opportunity to see their families follow Jesus too. He knew that other people would look to see if Christians really were as different as Jesus was. Silas also knew that everyone would need someone to look up to.

Being an example is always an adventure. It means you're serious about your faith. It means others might just have a reason to discover Jesus. *Like you did.*

You have a plan for my life, God.
Help me learn the plan by reading Your Word.

SIMEON

There was a man in Jerusalem by the name of Simeon.
He was a good man.
LUKE 2:25

Simeon followed God, but he also waited. He was promised that he would see the Messiah, God's own Son. He'd waited a long time, and he was old.

One day Simeon went to the temple. He worshipped God. He also looked around. Maybe this would be the promised day. *It was.*

Joseph and Mary took baby Jesus to the temple. He was eight days old. He was a baby, but He would grow up. He would die on a cross. He would save humans from the outcome of their sin. He rose again. Simeon knew God's good news before others. He looked at Jesus and said, "My eyes have seen the One Who will save men from the punishment of their sins" (Luke 2:30).

Simeon knew Jesus came for everyone. God kept His promise—He allowed Simeon to see God's Son. Simeon was close to the end of his earthly adventure, and God saved His best moment for him.

You want people to notice Your Son. He did the amazing.
He came to save people, God. He did just that. Thank You.

SIMON OF CYRENE

*They led Jesus away. A man named Simon was coming in
from the country of Cyrene and they made him
carry the cross following behind Jesus.*
Luke 23:26

You might think Simon had bad timing. He walked into Jerusalem when Jesus was walking to the cross. The trial was over. The verdict was made. Jesus had been beaten and was very weak. He struggled to carry the cross. People watched. Some made fun of Jesus. Simon? Just arrived.

Did he know Jesus? Was he just curious? Simon and his sons stood in the crowd and waited for Jesus to pass by. Maybe Jesus stumbled. Maybe He fell. A Roman soldier had seen enough. Simon was pulled from the crowd and forced to drag the cross through town for Jesus.

Maybe they spoke together. Maybe they didn't need to. Simon went from being a part of the crowd to being a participant in God's great rescue plan.

That day was one Simon never expected. He walked with Jesus when no one else would.

*It can seem hard to follow You when other people don't
think it makes sense. God, help me understand
You are the only One worth following.*

SIMON THE PHARISEE

One of the proud religious law-keepers wanted Jesus to eat with him. Jesus went to his house and sat down to eat.
LUKE 7:36

Israel seemed filled with *proud religious law-keepers* and *sinners*. The sinners didn't want to spend time with proud religious law-keepers because they just made them feel bad and offered no hope. The proud religious law-keepers didn't want to hang out with sinners because they broke God's law.

A man named Simon was a proud religious law-keeper. He invited Jesus to his house to eat. Maybe he wanted to know more about what Jesus taught. He hadn't expected a sinner to come into his house, but a woman who sinned came in and poured expensive perfume on Jesus' feet. It was her way of honoring Him. Simon had unkind thoughts. Jesus told Simon that when a person is forgiven, they love more. That's what had happened to this sinner. Simon struggled to accept Jesus' words.

It must have been a wonderful thing to see Jesus teach by doing and not just saying.

Thank You for Your forgiveness of my sins, God.
I need it. You offer it. I accept it. I love You.

SIMON THE SORCERER

A man by the name of Simon had done witchcraft there. The people of Samaria were surprised at the things he did. He pretended that he was a great man.

ACTS 8:9

Simon was a sorcerer in Samaria. He did things that amazed people. They couldn't believe what they were seeing. They thought he was a magician or something more. Simon liked when people thought he was really special.

Then Simon saw the apostle Philip do things that amazed him. Simon wanted what Philip had, so he said he wanted to follow God too. He wanted to impress more people with what he could do.

Then the apostles Peter and John came to town, and Simon saw more miracles that God did through these men. Now Simon was willing to pay money to buy this magic. Simon still didn't understand.

Jesus used miracles to help people and to show His power. Simon wanted to impress people and say that he was powerful. He needed to learn more. Simon wasn't thinking right.

You are powerful, God. Help me remember that. Please use me to help others. I want to honor You.

SIMON (PETER)

*Simon Peter has told how God first visited the people
who are not Jews. He was getting a people for Himself.*
ACTS 15:14

Simon was another name for Peter. His family was part of the people of Israel. He learned the law but struggled to remember that Jesus came to rescue *anyone*.

One day Simon had a dream. There were all kinds of animals that the people of Israel did not eat. They only ate foods they considered clean. In the dream God told Simon Peter to pick an animal and prepare it for a meal. The problem was that every animal he saw was considered unclean.

God helped Simon Peter learn that people who weren't from the family of Israel should not be considered unclean, because God could make them clean. They could be part of a bigger family—those who followed Jesus.

Simon Peter had the adventure of learning that God was so crazy in love with the world that He could take even the outcasts and make them part of His family.

*You don't keep out anyone who wants in, God.
Help me remember You do the impossible and
make any sinner a potential family member.*

SISERA

"I will have Sisera, the head of Jabin's army, meet you at the river Kishon. He will have his war-wagons and his many soldiers with him. But I will give him into your hand."
JUDGES 4:7

Maybe you've played a sport where people pick who they want on their team. No one likes to be picked last. Usually one team has more experienced players. That's never fun for the other team.

Sisera was certain he had the best team, but it wasn't a game. It was a battle Sisera was willing to fight. He was certain the Hebrews couldn't find enough soldiers to succeed, but God picked the Hebrews, and He was always their best leader. He promised a Hebrew win.

Sisera led by physical strength and personal planning. God led by a strength Sisera could never understand. God led by a plan Sisera never expected.

When Sisera thought he had an easy win, God used a woman named Jael to defeat him with the offer of shelter and a glass of milk.

God can use anything and anyone He wants to get His job done.

I always want to remember that when I'm on Your team, I win, God.

SOLOMON

*Solomon sat on the throne of his father David
and things went well for the nation.*
1 KINGS 2:12

.... ☆ ....

Solomon wasn't the oldest son of King David. He wasn't the strongest. He wasn't the best looking. But he would become Israel's king. David said so. God said so. Solomon knew he had a lot to learn.

Then? Solomon had a dream. In that dream God offered him a gift. He could have whatever he wanted. A lot of thoughts must have been running through his mind, but Solomon knew that if he was going to be a good king, he would need wisdom. That's the gift he asked for. God said that Solomon could have asked for things like a long life or loads of money. God thought Solomon's choice was perfect. God gave him wisdom and all the good gifts that come with being wise.

Solomon was going on a new adventure. Being a king was a big responsibility. Becoming wise helped him protect his people.

*Help me want to be wise more than I want to be rich,
God. Help me choose to learn from You
over anything else I could want.*

STEPHEN

*They chose Stephen who was a man full
of faith and full of the Holy Spirit.*
ACTS 6:5

After Jesus went back to heaven, the church began to grow. People believed what they heard about Jesus, and each began their own adventure with Him. *That was very good.*

As the church grew, more help was needed. One of the first men who was asked to help was Stephen. Because Stephen was full of faith and power, the religious leaders didn't like him. People argued with Stephen. The religious leaders looked for people willing to say bad things about Stephen. The religious leaders said bad things about Stephen. When Stephen tried to help them understand the truth about Jesus, they got angry. They picked up stones and threw them at Stephen.

It was a sad day when Stephen died this way. But Stephen knew Jesus. He knew why he followed Jesus. And Stephen knew that when he died, he would meet Jesus. *That was very good.*

*It's sad when bad things happen to good people, God.
It doesn't seem fair. But You overcome trouble and
promise a place where I can be with You always.*

TATTENAI

Then Tattenai, the leader over the land on the other side of the River, and Shethar-bozenai, and their friends, came to them and said, "Who told you to build on this house and to finish the building?"

EZRA 5:3

.... ☆ ....

King Darius said that he wanted the temple rebuilt in Jerusalem. He wasn't the king of Israel. He wasn't the king of Judah. The people of those nations had been taken prisoner. King Darius was now in charge of them. God gave him the desire to rebuild the temple. The people of Judah and Israel would come home, and the temple needed work.

Zerubbabel and Jeshua were in charge of the work. One day they had a visitor. Tattenai lived in a country nearby. When he found out they were rebuilding, he demanded to know why. He sent a letter to the king. He thought the men would get in trouble. Instead, the king asked Tattenai to help them by making sure they had enough food and supplies. That wasn't the response Tattenai expected.

Let me learn what I need to learn instead of doing what I should have avoided, God. May I always seek the truth.

TERAH

*When Terah had lived seventy years,
he became the father of Abram.*
GENESIS 11:26

Who was Abram's dad? If you said Terah, then you probably read the verse above or maybe you're just really smart. Terah's name means "wild goat," but Terah seemed to care deeply for his family and to help when he could.

There was a time when he proved his willingness to help. Terah moved with Abram and his wife, Sarai, to a place called Haran in the land of Canaan. Terah continued to spend time with his son. When Terah died, God called Abram to a new land.

Some people think Terah was a wicked man who followed many gods. While the Bible doesn't say for sure, we do know that Terah's son Abram followed the one true God and would become the father of a great nation.

Maybe Terah thought that adventure was travel and exploration. God proved to Terah's son Abram that adventure was anywhere God was.

I want to live my life knowing that my greatest adventures happen as I follow You, even if I never leave the town I was raised in. God, help me follow You wherever You lead.

TERTULLUS

*They brought in Paul. Then Tertullus started
to tell what the Jews had against him.*
ACTS 24:2

Maybe you've watched a courtroom drama on television. The judge listens to two lawyers. One lawyer defends the person accused of a crime, and the other lawyer explains why he or she thinks the accused actually committed the crime.

Tertullus would have been one of those lawyers. Felix arrived to hear the arguments against Paul. Tertullus told Felix that Paul caused trouble everywhere he went, that he was a leader of those who followed Jesus, and that he had no respect for the temple. Tertullus may not have investigated the stories. He may have just said what he had been told to say.

Tertullus wasn't even hired by the government. He was hired by Jewish people who just didn't like Paul. His argument wasn't true.

Tertullus was smart and could talk like a lawyer, but those skills didn't end in adventure. He wasn't seeking truth but merely a paycheck.

*It could be easy to think a job is more important
than You, God. Help me remember You have
always been able to take care of me.*

173

THEOPHILUS

Dear Theophilus, I have looked with care into these things from the beginning. I have decided it would be good to write them to you one after the other the way they happened.
LUKE 1:3

Did you know that the books of Luke and Acts were written to a man named Theophilus? He would have been the first to read about Jesus' birth the way Luke wrote it. He would have read all the stories of the church after Jesus rose from the dead.

God wanted these words written, but Theophilus may have been used by God to help Luke understand the value of writing these books of history.

Some think that Theophilus was a lawyer in Paul's trial with Felix. They think he asked Luke for these documents so they could be given to Felix. These books would show the history of Jesus and the history of Paul. We don't know that they were used this way, but they do show the good things God did, and they are evidence for people today asking questions about Jesus and His family.

I want to read Your Word so I can learn the truth of Your goodness, God.

THIEF ON THE CROSS

"We are suffering and we should, because of the wrong we have done. But this Man has done nothing wrong."
LUKE 23:41

Dying on a cross happened to criminals—not to people who had done nothing wrong. That's probably why many struggled with seeing Jesus hanging on a cross.

There were three crosses on a hill the day Jesus died. One criminal made fun of Jesus. He didn't believe Jesus had power to help. The other criminal was different. He knew he had done wrong. He knew God was right. He also knew that Jesus had done nothing wrong.

The second criminal knew he was suffering for doing the wrong thing, but Jesus was suffering even though He had done nothing wrong. The religious leaders would have heard this man's words. Roman soldiers would have heard those words. Jesus heard those words, and He said, "Today you will be with Me in Paradise" (Luke 23:43).

This criminal found the adventure of freedom at the end of his life because he believed the Freedom Giver.

*Help me remember that what You offer is freedom, Lord.
I want to walk with You and away from sin.*

THOMAS

[Jesus] said to Thomas, "Put your finger into My hands.
Put your hand into My side. Do not doubt, believe!"
JOHN 20:27

Hebrews 11 is the "Faith Hall of Fame." It makes sense to learn what faith means through the words in this book. "Faith is being sure we will get what we hope for. It is being sure of what we cannot see" (Hebrews 11:1).

Thomas learned from Jesus for three years. When Jesus died on the cross, Thomas must have given up all hope. When the other disciples told Thomas they had seen Jesus, he didn't believe it.

Eventually Thomas saw Jesus after He had risen from the dead. Jesus insisted that Thomas inspect His wounds. He told him that belief should replace doubt. Then Jesus said something that sounds a lot like it would fit in the Faith Hall of Fame: "Those are happy who have never seen Me and yet believe!" (John 20:29).

I can be a lot like Thomas, Lord. I can say I believe and then
say, "I'll believe it when I see it." Help me believe
what You say even if I have to wait to see it.

TIMOTHY

Paul went down to the cities of Derbe and Lystra.
There was a follower there named Timothy.
Acts 16:1

.... ☆ ....

If you have ever heard the word *mentor*, then you know it means someone who's willing to teach someone what they know. Maybe you learned something from a mentor today.

Mentors don't *have* to teach—they want to. Paul was a mentor to Timothy. There was a time when Timothy would have been an outcast. His father was Greek.

Good news—Jesus came for everyone, so Timothy was welcome in the church. He became a leader in the church. Paul taught. Timothy learned. Paul took missionary trips. Timothy followed. Paul asked other people to help Timothy. They helped him.

It is good for someone your age to know that God can take a young man and help him become useful, faithful, and honorable.

Timothy started a great adventure when he understood that God was for him—not against him. He could be confident walking forward because God brought Paul to walk with him.

Help me find someone who can help teach me, God.
When they teach, help me learn. When You lead,
keep my feet moving in Your direction.

177

TITUS

I am writing to you, Titus. You are my true son in the faith which we both have. May you have loving-favor and peace from God the Father and Jesus Christ, the One Who saves.
TITUS 1:4

Titus also was mentored by the apostle Paul. Less is written about Titus than Timothy, but it seems Titus was very good at bringing people together. He helped deliver God's plan to people and then helped them learn how to follow that plan.

Paul helped Titus learn how Christian leaders should act, what they should do, and what makes a good church leader. This was important because churches needed to know what to expect from those who lead.

Paul relied on Timothy. Paul relied on Titus. Paul told the people of Corinth, "Titus works with me to help you" (2 Corinthians 8:23).

Don't be surprised if you begin to think you have to do everything on your own. That was never God's plan, though. Paul always had people he worked with. Jesus had twelve disciples. He wants you to have someone to help you too.

Let me help others, God. Let others help me.
Let me be part of Your team.

TUBAL-CAIN

*Zillah gave birth to Tubal-cain who
made things from brass and iron.*
GENESIS 4:22

Some believe Tubal-cain was the world's first blacksmith. He did a kind of work no one had ever seen before. He could take rocks (called ore) and melt them down in a fire. Some think he was the one who discovered how to make metal. He was good at his job. He was considered strong and important.

The adventure of Tubal-cain was one of invention. He used his imagination to make things no one had ever seen before. He made things that were useful. He made things that were decorative. He made things for battle. He probably even made things he just thought were fun to make.

God wants you to use the things you learn and link them, like a chain, to what you are willing to do for Him. He loves to take the things you are passionate about and make them useful to someone else. He made you for a purpose. Let Him find a way to make you useful.

*Being useful to You sounds like a good idea, Lord.
Take what I know and use it to do what You need done.*

UNNAMED BOY (FISH)

"There is a boy here who has five loaves of barley bread and two small fish. What is that for so many people?"
JOHN 6:9

Can you imagine being part of an event and having thousands of people show up? You're happy so many came, but no one brought food, and you don't have any. The organizer of the event asks you to feed them all. What do you do?

Jesus knew what this was like. He had been speaking, and the people kept coming to hear Him. More than five thousand people showed up. There were no drive-through restaurants, the disciples didn't have enough money to feed the people, and everyone was hungry. All they could find was a boy with a lunch that included some bread and fish. Jesus said it was enough. The boy saw his lunch feed all the people with a dozen baskets left over.

One boy with one lunch fed thousands. That was a fish story he could share for the rest of his life—and his story was true.

> *You make miracles happen every day, God. Help me look for them. I want to thank You for them and share them with others.*

URIAH THE HITTITE

Joab's brother Asahel was among the thirty. . . .
And there was. . .Uriah the Hittite.
2 SAMUEL 23:24, 38–39

There are different branches of the military. The members of each one are trained and ready so when they're needed they can help immediately. King David had these kinds of soldiers. The Bible calls them "the three" and "the thirty."

These were mighty men who had proven they knew what to do and when to do it. Uriah the Hittite was one of these soldiers. He was an honorable man and one of King David's best soldiers.

Uriah had been loyal to David even before he became king.

Being loyal is an adventure, and Uriah proved especially trustworthy. He understood responsibility. It was a choice he made.

You can be loyal too. Start with God. Include your family, your church, and your friends. Prove to be trustworthy, patient, and kind. If you make promises, keep them. Loyalty is just what God offers you. Act like Him.

Help me stick to Your side, God. I don't want to
abandon those You bring to me as friends
and family. Help me be loyal.

UZZAH

They carried the special box of God on a new wagon,
and brought it out of the family of Abinadab which
was on the hill. Abinadab's sons Uzzah and
Ahio were leading the new wagon.

2 Samuel 6:3

································· ·································

God's special box was called the "ark of the covenant." A covenant is a promise.

God told Moses to build the special box. Many years passed. The holy ark had been kept away from God's people for too long. King David wanted the ark back. People sang and danced as it moved down the hill.

The rules hadn't changed. No one was supposed to touch the special box. *No one.* Anyone who touched it would die.

Uzzah and his brother Ahio were pulling the special box in a wagon. Uzzah noticed the special box tipping. He reached out his hand to steady the "never touch" box. Uzzah died. The crowd was sad. The singing stopped.

There can be joy in knowing that when Jesus died for your sins, His *new* covenant made it possible to have sins forgiven. Rejoice.

I am grateful You forgive sin, God. Thanks for welcoming
me to Your side even after I break Your rules.

UZZIAH

*Then all the people took Uzziah,
who was sixteen years old, and made him king.*
2 Chronicles 26:1

King Uzziah began ruling Judah by making good decisions. He was well known and highly respected. He was considered one of the best kings in the history of Judah.

In the second half of Uzziah's reign, he made a decision that changed everything. God's Word says that the king became very proud. No one could tell him what to do. He thought he was strong and wise. He thought his ideas were best. One day King Uzziah walked into the temple and burned incense he created. God had made rules about the type of incense He wanted. Uzziah didn't care.

The priests told the king this was wrong. Uzziah left the temple with a skin disease that meant he had to stay in a house away from the palace. He couldn't go to God's house anymore. His adventure was set aside the day he thought he was smarter than God.

*You want me to pay attention to where I'm going,
God. I want to know Your good plans and
obey Your directions every day of my life.*

WISE MEN

Soon after Jesus was born, some wise men who learned things from stars came to Jerusalem from the East.
MATTHEW 2:1

The men had studied old papers with ancient writing. They found the bits and pieces that connected the signs in the sky with the birth of an important king. They weren't sure if the child was being celebrated as king in the faraway land, but they gathered together and made the long journey to see the child. They brought gifts because they were certain they would find Him. *They would.*

They stopped to see King Herod. If anyone knew where to find this new king, it would be the man who sat on the throne. He didn't know about the new king, but he was very jealous.

They found the boy, Jesus, in Bethlehem. They worshipped the new king and gave Him gifts. Then they said goodbye and returned to their books in the East. They had met the child—God's own Son. They honored this King. Jesus became part of their story.

*I am glad my life came in contact with Yours, God.
Help me keep Your story a part of mine.*

ZACCHEUS

Zaccheus wanted to see Jesus but he could not because so many people were there and he was a short man.
LUKE 19:3

················· ☆ ·················

Zaccheus wanted to meet Jesus. He was coming to town and everyone would show up to see Him, talk to Him, or pray for a miracle.

Zaccheus would be happy just to see Him, but everyone was taller than he was. He found the answer on the limb of a tree. He could see very well. He watched the crowd. Then he spotted Jesus. Soon Jesus would walk under the tree and Zaccheus would climb down and go back to being a tax collector.

Wait. Jesus stopped. He looked up. He spoke a name—and it was the name *Zaccheus.* Jesus spoke to him and asked him to come down. Jesus wanted to share a meal with him.

Spending time with Jesus meant Zaccheus changed how he collected taxes and made up for what he had wrongfully taken. Jesus wanted him to be different. Zaccheus wanted to be more like Jesus.

Help me become more like You, God.
I don't think it will be easy, but I know You will help me.

185

ZACHARIAS

*Zacharias was doing his work as a
religious leader for God.*
LUKE 1:8

Zacharias had heard the stories of Abraham and was familiar with the messenger prophet Samuel. Abraham had a son when he was old. Samuel was born to a family that wanted children.

Zacharias and his wife were getting older. They had never had children and weren't sure they would ever hear a child's voice say "Papa" or "Mama."

Zacharias was a priest. He made the best of the work God had given him to do. He was faithful to do the work, but he didn't trust God's message. An angel told Zacharias he would be a dad. He had always prayed for a child, but could this be true? The old priest questioned God. But because it was God who made the promise, He made Zacharias unable to speak until the boy was born. That boy's name was John the Baptist.

Zacharias was offered an adventure in trusting God for what was coming up. The priest found it easier to trust God about what had already happened.

*I need to believe You have great adventures coming up,
God. Help me think past the last lesson You taught.*

SCRIPTURE INDEX

OLD TESTAMENT

Genesis
2:7. 15
4:3. 34
4:4 9
4:22 179
5:24 50
5:27. 121
6:8. 131
7:13 160
10:8. 130
11:26 172
12:1 10
13:5. 110
16:15 71
17:5 11
24:10. 12
25:30 53
28:20–21 75
31:2 105
32:28 72
35:24 31
37:22 150
37:26–27 101

39:1 . . . . .96, 146
40:1. 140
40:5 39
41:52. 52

Exodus
1:11. 139
3:1 86
3:11 123
4:27 7
17:12 68
38:22 32

Numbers
13:30. 35
16:1 104
22:21. 25

Deuteronomy
1:38. 132

Joshua
24:15. 99

Judges
3:15 45
4:7. 168
4:14. 27
6:12 62
11:1. 84
13:2 115
13:24 153

Ruth
4:13 33
4:21 134

1 Samuel
2:34 66
3:6. 46
3:19 154
9:17 156
13:14 42
19:2 95
21:9 17
21:10 14

2 Samuel
6:3. 182
9:6. 120
12:1 125
15:13 13

19:32 30
23:24, 38–39 181

1 Kings
2:12 169
11:43 149
15:14 23
18:3 133
18:22 47
22:7 82

2 Kings
5:1 124
7:3–4 67
8:4 49
10:28 83
12:2 88
18:3 65
18:18 87
18:28 148
20:4 70
22:2 100

1 Chronicles
4:9 74
12:32 73
16:7 24
27:33 69

2 Chronicles
23:16. 81
31:13 85
26:1 183

Ezra
1:2 40
5:3. 171
7:6. 58

Nehemiah
1:1. 128
4:1 155

Esther
2:8. 55
2:22. 122
3:5. 63

Job
1:1. 89
2:11 48

Proverbs
31:1 109

Ecclesiastes
9:15. 145

Ezekiel
2:1 57

Daniel
1:15 8
3:13. 159
3:28 127
6:3. 41

Joel
1:1. 90

Amos
1:1. 18

Jonah
1:1–3 94

NEW TESTAMENT

Matthew
1:16 97
2:1 184
9:9. 116
14:28. 138
17:1. 91
27:2. 144

27:57	98	23:41	175
		24:18	37

Mark

1:16	20	**John**	
1:19	79	1:6–7	93
2:3	136	1:45	126
3:18–19	78	3:1–2	129
3:19	102	6:9	180
10:22	151	9:1	114
10:46	29	11:5	107
15:21	152	18:10	113
		20:27	176

Luke

1:3	174	**Acts**	
1:8	186	1:13	103
2:8	161	1:26	117
2:25	163	3:5	106
3:38	158	5:34	61
7:3	36	6:5	170
7:36	165	8:3	157
8:19	77	8:9	166
8:41	76	8:26	142
15:20	147	8:38	54
16:20	108	9:17	19
17:15	64	10:22	38
19:3	185	11:24	28
23:17	26	12:25	92
23:26	164	15:14	167

15:32	162	Hebrews
16:1	177	7:2–3 118
16:27	143	11:3 119
17:6–7	80	
17:22	137	3 John
17:34	44	1:12 43
18:24	21	
20:9	56	
21:10	16	
24:2	173	
24:10	59	
24:22	112	
26:24	60	

Romans
16:3 22

Colossians
1:7 51
4:14 111

Titus
1:4 178

Philemon
1:1 141
1:10 135

MORE GREAT RESOURCES FOR BRAVE BOYS!

100 Adventurous Stories for Brave Boys
Boys are history-makers! And this deeply compelling storybook proves it! Just for boys in your life, this collection of 100 adventurous stories of Christian men—from the Bible, history, and today—will empower them to know and understand how men of great character have made an impact in the world and how much smaller our faith (and the biblical record) would be without them.

Hardback / 978-1-64352-356-9 / $16.99

A to Z Devotions for Brave Boys
What makes a brave boy of God? . . . Boys ages 5 and up will discover the answers in this delightful A to Z devotional! *A to Z Devotions for Brave Boys* introduces boys to a positive character trait for every letter of the alphabet alongside an inspiring devotional reading.

Hardback / 978-1-64352-515-0 / $14.99